CONTENTS

W0009735

INTRODUCTION

This is the story of my life and covers the forty-seven years I worked with the railways, starting in 1947 as a junior clerk, at the age of fourteen years old, on a snowy February morning at Carlisle Citadel Station, wearing my very first pair of long trousers and old school cap, with the London Midland and Scottish Railway Company.

Trains were all steam hauled and there were no problems caused by "wrong type of snow" or "leaves on the line," these were totally unheard of. The trains were heated by steam and were always warm and the coaches were either corridor or non-corridor type. Carlisle Citadel Station was an exceedingly busy, important station, with seven different companies using it before nationalisation in 1948, when it became British Railways. It was used then by North British, North Eastern, Midland Railway, London North Western, Glasgow and South Western, Caledonian Railway, and last, but not least, the lovely little local, Maryport and Carlisle Railway.

There were no diesel locomotives (DMUs - Diesel Motor Units), ticket machines, pay trains, power signal boxes, area managers, passenger's friend, buffet cars, passenger trolleys, electric locomotives, Dr Beeching, John Major's passenger charter or seat reservations. How we ever managed to run a railway before these you may ask, but we did with great success! Every station had its own station master and full staff of booking clerks, porters, guards etc whatever the size and open stations were unheard of.

I have been in my time a platform porter, station porter, left luggage attendant, passenger shunter, passenger guard, crossing keeper, station foreman, senior railman, chargeman and finally, supervisor, spending my years at Burneside, Kendal, Morecambe and finally to Oxenholme. I have learned a lot, experienced all the difficulties at first hand, seen a side of life and people I could never have dreamed of meeting in any other type of job and have tried to portray my railway days as humorous, interesting and informative as possible. I always used to say to my workmates or family after another particular incident had happened, that would leave me shaking my head in disbelief, "I could write a book!" So that is precisely what I have done and I have tried to make it as accurate as I can possibly remember, so please forgive me if I have made any slight errors along the way.

I am now retired and live happily at Arnside with my wife on the beautiful Kent Estuary. We are now great grandparents and time is spent visiting family, friends and colleagues we have made during the years and at times just sitting quietly thinking back to my days on the railways and how it used to be in the 'great days of steam'. I hope you enjoy my book as much as I have enjoyed writing it. My thanks to Preston Whiteley, Alec Mayor, Robert Leslie, Percy Duff, John Bateson, Harold Bowtell and Jay Hartley who kindly loaned illustrations. I am grateful for the help and guidance of John Marsh, to Anne Bonney for compiling the book and my friend Ken Bateson for his help. Let me now share my memories with you.

John Cottam 1999

Princess Louise 'Class 7' No 46201 and a Class 40 Diesel, on platform 3, at Carlisle Citadel Station, taken on 27 August 1960.
Derek Singleton   Preston Whiteley Collection

WHERE I HAVE LIVED AND WORKED

1947 - 1951   Worked as a junior clerk in the district goods and passenger manager's office and in the accounts office for London Midland and Scottish Railway Company

1951 - 1954   National Service for the Government

1954 - 1961   Worked in Carlisle Station, from porter, leading parcel porter, shunter to passenger guard for British Rail

1961 - 1971   Crossing keeper, Burneside; station foreman, Kendal Station for British Rail

1971 - 1976   Passenger guard, Morecambe Promenade Station for British Rail

1976 - 1995   General relief, senior railman, chargeman, supervisor, Oxenholme Station for British Rail until retirement

Carnforth Station Staff in 1914 - Joint London & North Western, Furness & Midland Railways
Left to right - front row: T. Clement, N. Iniff, J. Jackson, W. H. Owen, R. Jackson, R. Sanderson, T. Atkinson and T. Clark
Back row: N. Wilkinson, Richard Cottam (my father), G. Norman, J. Owen (Station Master),
H. Farrer, R. Duckett, G. Taylor, T. Dinsdale, W. Gibbins and J. Fawcett
Mayoh Press Ltd, Carnforth

Chapter One
MY FAMILY

I was born on 15 November 1932 at 12.20 pm, one of identical twin boys, at 33 Borland Avenue, Botcherby, Carlisle, and christened John Alan Cottam. (I was told I had been christened, John, after two brothers who were partners at the local doctor's surgery where my mother attended and, of course, my grandfather was also called, John). My brother, William, or Bill as he is called, was born twenty minutes earlier. My mother, Helena Mary Ormond was born at Quernmore, near Lancaster in 1897 and my father, Richard Cottam, was born at Carnforth in 1896, both Lancastrians. I have also an older sister, Lorna, who was born in 1920 and older brother Duncan, who was born in 1922.

My mother met my father in 1913, when she was working in the refreshment room, on Lancaster Railway Station and father at this time was working as a junior porter on the railway, at Bolton-le-Sands, before going to Carnforth. My father came from a railway family and had started his railway career there in 1910, as a boy of sixteen. His brother, John was an engine driver, his eldest son, Ken, was an engine fitter, his other son Richard was a fireman and all were based at Carnforth.

My mother and father were married in 1919, just after the end of the First World War. Father was in the Kings Own Regiment in the war and told me of being in the trenches in Mons, Belgium, where he was wounded and lost two of his middle fingers on his right hand. Lorna and Duncan were born at 'Rock House', Crag Bank, Carnforth and my grandmother used to farm at 'Newfields', Crag Bank. In 1924 our family moved from Carnforth, Lancashire, over the border into Scotland, to Gretna. Father was a travelling ticket collector in those days.

In 1929 the family moved again, this time back over the border to Carlisle, where father had become a guard, he worked most of his time on the Midland Railway. He always used to joke with his mates that he worked the 'premier railway' and I must say I agreed with him. Everyone knows it today as the Settle and Carlisle Railway but it will always be the Midland Railway to me.

My father knew every station and signal box between Carlisle and London St Pancras on that line. There were two routes to London, one via Leeds, Sheffield Trent and Leicester and the other via Nottingham and Derby. Even through the middle of the night my father knew where he was, if the train should slow down, even without glancing out of the window. Remarkable you might say, but I should imagine it took years to get that perfect, but they were a different breed of men in those days, not many colour light signals and certainly no telephones every 200 yards. It was a perfection I later tried to live up to but I am afraid I did not even come near!

My father compiled a book from memory, which I still proudly keep in my possession, of the two routes from Carlisle to London, listing in order every siding, signal box, station and every other item of interest. I helped him a little with it, even before I started myself on the railway and I know for certain that all the other guards borrowed it from him to copy because it was all planned very simply and was easy to follow.

Father used to tell me about the early railway barracks, these were really like hostels, where drivers, firemen and guards could sleep, after working trains to London from Carlisle for example, as it took eight hours or more to get there then, so they had to rest before returning. These railway barracks were situated all over the country. They comprised of a canteen, recreation rooms, bedrooms with just a single bed, chair, a small dressing table, all very warm and comfortable in their own way.

My father used to sleep in Kentish Town barracks every other week for years, travelling over night from Carlisle. He did this right through the Second World War. Many's the time he used to tell us he had to sleep under the table in the canteen, not daring to go up to his room. This was when the Germans started bombing London during daylight hours and then, of course, he had to work his train back to Carlisle at night. I often used to notice how tired he sometimes looked, when he arrived home the following morning. Father always counted himself pretty lucky and I think he was. I remember him telling me one of his experiences in London, when his train had just left platform 13 at St Pancras, when five minutes later this platform received a direct hit by a German bomb. He confessed the fact later, that he often worried whether he would ever see his home again when he went on these London trips.

The house I was born in at 33 Borland Avenue, Botcherby, Carlisle, was a council house and I later learned from my father how we came to get it. He had been working the 21.05 hrs train from London St Pancras, when he was approached at St Pancras by a well dressed gentleman, who asked him where he was working the train to, to which my father promptly told him, "Carlisle!" He then said that the gentleman had told him that he had been unable to book a sleeper and would it be possible for him to have a first class compartment, as he required to do some urgent paperwork and also get some much needed sleep. My father told him that this wasn't a problem and showed him straight away to a compartment and assured him that he would not be disturbed. Next morning, when the train was approaching Carlisle, this same gentleman came into my father's van to thank him for the pleasant journey he had had and asked

Down

CARLISLE No.4B
No.5

MILE POSTS

London Rd Jct. LNE

Pt Perl Bdg Jct
Pt Perl Goods

Durran Hill Jct.

Durran Hill South Sdgs

SCOTBY 5

COMMUNICATION

Howe + Co's Sidings

308 — All except up Advance Starter

307 — NOT TRACKED only down Starter

NOT " (Signals independent down goods line only)

301 — NOT TRACKED only Starter

306 — 466 yds NORTH of Station 1 in 132 all except Down, No Block MARKER or Staff

305 — 690 yds outside up Home Signal 1 in 134 NOT TRACKED

304 —

303 — NOT TRACKED only Down Advance Starter

Copy of Carlisle section out of my father's handbook.

whether he had far to go home. My father told him that he lived at Gretna, which was approximately ten miles away and that he cycled to and from work, which was not unusual in those days.

At this point the gentleman produced his card and told my father to contact his office as soon as possible regarding being allocated a newly built council house. The gentleman was no other than the housing manager for Carlisle City Council. My parents could hardly believe their good fortune and next day called at his office, where the secretary handed over the keys to 33 Borland Ave, Carlisle, for them to go and view and see if it was suitable. This was done in appreciation for what my father had done and as the housing manager he did not see why my father should have to travel all that distance in all weathers, after working all night. What a nice way to say thank you!

He also told me about the time he worked as guard on the royal train, when he took the Queen and Duke of Edinburgh, part of their journey to Leeds. He was taken off his normal duties at least three weeks before and tested on all the rules and regulations appertaining to running of trains and anything else they could think of, to cover all possible contingencies. He had to quote every signal, siding, station, tunnels, gradients etc, between Carlisle and Leeds. He was also supplied with a complete new uniform, new flags, new hand lamp, down to new whistle! On the big day itself, he said, that he was just more or less a passenger as he put it, there appeared to be a person to cover every rule in the book, in fear of anything going wrong. He also used to say, that whenever the Queen travelled by train, there was a policeman on every bridge the train went under, from London to Scotland. Whenever Royal Trains passed through stations they had to be immaculate, all barrows, parcel mail bags or anything unnecessary had to be hidden away. Everything had to be 'tip top' as the saying goes!

I started school when I was five years old with Bill and we went to Norman Street, in Greystone Road, Carlisle and we were there until we left at eleven, to go to Brook Street Secondary School. Lorna had gone to Margaret Sewells for girls and Duncan to Creightons School for boys, having both passed their eleven plus exams.

I remember Bill and I myself when we were about ten, going down to the railway bridge at Botcherby and writing down all the train engine numbers. It wasn't called 'train spotting' in those days, it was 'engine numbers' and of course it was all steam trains and we would stand there for three or four hours at a time on weekends and holidays. It was the Midland and North Eastern trains that passed under our bridge. To see other trains we had to go to Carlisle Citadel Station, which was just a bit further up the road. During the war I remember seeing tanks and guns being moved by train.

During 1944 and 1945, towards the end of the Second World War, my education at school consisted of only half days at school. This was to accommodate the influx of evacuees, from places like Coventry and London and they brought some of their own teachers with them.

When I used to go on my holidays to my granny's farm at Carnforth, it was the 8.20 am London train I caught with the family. I remember it used to call at nearly every station between Carlisle and London, places like Shap, Tebay, Burton and Holme, Milnthorpe, Hest Bank, Garstang and the train did not arrive in London until 4.30 pm. I remember when we used to stand at Carnforth Station waiting for the train to take us back to Carlisle and the porter would shout at the top of his voice, "Oxenholme, Tebay, Penrith and Carlisle train."

There was a lot of publicity surrounding the film 'Brief Encounter' which featured the refreshment room at Carnforth Station in 1949, and the famous station clock. Now, the clock is all that is left in the derelict station. The original plaque that had been put up to commemorate the film had been removed and a new plaque has been presented by a young star from the film. An old friend who

Me and Bill in our best clothes, aged ten.

worked at Carnforth Station during this time, told me that it had been filmed during the night and he remembers all the stars, particularly Celia Johnson, Trevor Howard and Stanley Holloway. He particularly remembers Stanley Holloway and how he had been very nervous doing the scene where he had to cross the lines from one platform to the other, which was over the two main lines and was very relieved when he reached the other platform opposite the refreshment room. One can see why he had just been a little nervous!

By coincidence, not to help matters at this time, there had been a very large fire at the oil dump, in the sidings and a number of fire engines attended, as well as a fire fighting train, which had been sent for from Horwich. It was quite a sight and took some time to get the fire under control.

During the Second World War, the refreshment room at Carnforth Station was partitioned in two, one half being used for the serving of refreshments and the other half by the WRVS who prepared them for the soldiers who travelled on the troop trains. They were continually running short of cups as they were not always returned. In desperation, they put out requests and advertisements in the local press for anything that would hold tea, even jam jars were used!

The famous clock at Carnforth Station. It featured in the film, 'Brief Encounter'.
Photo taken 1998

Chapter Two
EARLY DAYS AT CARLISLE CITADEL STATION

When I left school at fourteen in December 1946, it was a foregone conclusion that I would join the railways, we were a railway family and indeed I had never thought of doing anything else. On 23 February 1947, I commenced as a junior clerk, in the district goods and passenger manager's office, at Carlisle Citadel Railway Station. I remember it well, there was a thick covering of snow on the ground and I reported for duty at 9 am sharp, to the chief accounts clerk, Horace Turner, wearing my very first pair of long trousers and school cap. I can't remember ever applying for the job, as far as I can recollect, my father had just put my name down and this was it. I don't even think I was interviewed or even seen beforehand, just given a date to start.

I worked for London Midland and Scottish and didn't wear a uniform as I was in one of the offices. My job consisted solely of receiving the account returns from the stations under the jurisdiction of the district goods and passenger manager's office, such places as Dunragit, Tarff, Maxwelltown, and Kirkinner, plus many more that I had never heard tell of but was very quickly going to learn. Our area took in stations as far away as Stranraer to the west and down as far as Appleby, in Westmorland, as it was then.

I worked in an office on the top floor looking out onto Court Square, so I had a good view of that busy area of Carlisle. To railwaymen, our office was also known as the 'outstanding department' as we dealt with all the unpaid bills. We received returns for goods, passenger and demurrage. Demurrage was another name given for rent, which was incurred for storing coal in the railway goods yards and this was paid by the local coal merchants who used these facilities. One of my first jobs was putting the receipts into date order and filing them. If a return had not been received from a particular station, a reminder was sent at the end of the month, if they had still failed to respond, a fortnight later we would telephone them.

In Carlisle itself, there were a number of offices, as it was a main station. There were two large refreshment rooms open 24 hrs a day, John Menzies had a large book stall, there was a railway canteen for the staff and in the corridor opposite this was a very large fish house (fish stored here awaiting collection by the fish mongers). There was even a signal box inside the station, two large parcel offices, for collection and sending, left luggage, lamp rooms (for trains - mostly red rear tail lights). Booking offices, two time offices, one for locomotives and one for traffic staff and, of course, waiting rooms and toilets.

The chief account's clerk at this time, as I said, was Horace Turner, a bachelor and very fastidious he was too. He had a love of the theatre and amateur dramatics. Joyce Tiffin was his typist. Tommy Brennan, was in charge of the claims office and was always very cheerful and Jean Mark was one of his female assistants. He had a saying, "Hey lads, get sticks!" I never did understand the meaning behind that, I don't know if anybody else did either! Jimmy O'Hagan was the boss in the staff office and Mary Muse and Alec Clarke were two of his assistants and I also remember working alongside, Jackie Liddle, Edwin Day and Robert Armstrong.

The district goods and passenger manager himself, was a Mr R Clarke and Mr Dempster was his assistant, but in 1948 after the railways were nationalised this was renamed the district traffic superintendent and Mr J A K Gray held this post and later, Mr T P Strafford. I remember the latter, as being a gentleman farmer type of character. He used to tell his staff that they didn't need to make an appointment to see him, they could just knock on his door and they could discuss their problem then and there. In a morning you used to hear him singing, 'To be a farmer's boy'. He was later promoted to chief of operations for the whole of the Midlands.

I remember a guard from Carlisle telling me the story, of how he had met him at 2 am on a very cold winter's morning when he had gone into his guard's van. His train had been standing in Derby Station and he had said to the guard, "My, my, it's cold in here!" To which the guard had replied, "Yes and how would you like to travel in this all the way to London from Carlisle? Worse still, I will have to travel back in it!" Mr Strafford then replied, "You won't have to, if I have anything to do with it!" The guard left continuing his cold journey southwards to London, firmly believing Mr Strafford would have forgotten all about his cold dilemma. He hadn't, for when he returned to his van that night at St Pancras, he found that it had been replaced by a brand new one, with overhead steam pipes, making all the difference in the world to his journey north. The guard could only smile in gratitude and say a big thank you to Mr Strafford, who had remembered after all! That was just one example of the sort of person he was and is remembered for!

In the 1940's, Carlisle Station had a station master, three assistants, four platform inspectors, three station foremen, senior porters, parcel porters and station porters, approximately one hundred in all. On top of that we had twelve shunters, three yard foremen, train announcers, lampmen and three time clerks, who were responsible for booking everyone on and off duty and at least forty guards who worked out of the station.

In these early days at Carlisle, the trains were all steam of course and there were seven different railway companies running into the station, all supposed to be in competition with one another but really working together - North British, North Eastern, Midland Railway, London North Western, Glasgow and South Western, Caledonian Railway, and last, but not least, the little Maryport and Carlisle Railway. It was a magical time for me working there, then, and I felt my life was just beginning and I was so proud to be a part of this world of trains.

Our first home at Cotehill in 1956.
Phyllis is in the front garden and the Settle
Carlisle line is in the foreground.

My two daughters, Denise and Nancy on
the stile outside our house waiting for me
to pass with my train to London.
This was taken about 1958.

Mother and father at my wedding.

Chapter Three
NATIONAL SERVICE AND LIVING AT COTEHILL

I went into the Royal Air Force in January 1951, to do my National Service along with my twin brother, Bill. We went to RAF Padgate, near Warrington. National Service was compulsory then and all young men were called up as soon as they were eighteen years old and did two years. During the first week at Warrington, we had our medical and were kitted out with our uniform. After this we started our eight week's training, or 'square bashing' as everyone called it. This included, marching, drilling, rifle training and assault courses. We were certainly fit at the end of it and of course it disciplined us. We were then posted to Liverpool. Our camp there, was the 6th floor of the Royal Liver Building, on the Pier Head and we actually lived over the River Mersey, in Wallasey. These were civilian billets. We worked on the Liverpool Docks acting as liaison officers for the United States Forces, checking all their stores etc as they came off the boats from America, bound for Sealand and Burtonwood USAF bases and other bases in Suffolk and Norfolk. I was called a surface movements clerk, which was roughly the equivalent to what I had been doing on the railways before I was called up. It was an experience I will never forget and was pleased when it was over.

During my time away I met and married a young nurse from Liverpool, called Phyllis. The RAF asked us all to stop for an extra year, but I didn't want to. Denise, our daughter was born on 11 February, 1953.

I started back at Carlisle Citadel Station, this time as a platform porter. My duties involved sweeping platforms, cleaning toilets, bill posting and any other duties as requested by the platform foreman. I generally worked on platform 1, though this sometimes changed. The uniform we wore was made from heavy, navy serge material. We had trousers, long sleeved waistcoats and jackets with silver buttons and heavy wool overcoats. We were not given footwear, shirts or ties, so it was left to us to decide what shirts or ties to wear. There was no strict regulation concerning uniform until the 1980's.

When we first came back to Carlisle we lived with my parents, at 33 Borland Avenue, Botcherby, Carlisle. For the next two years we continued there and Nancy our second daughter, was born on 2 June 1955, at the City General Hospital, Fusehill Street, Carlisle.

A few months after Nancy was born a cottage came up for let, this was to be our first home, a railway cottage at Cotehill Station, some nine and half miles from Carlisle. I had seen the advertisement for it in the Time Office at Carlisle Station.

The rent was five shillings a week, which was automatically docked off my wages. We moved in during February 1956 and it is situated on the beautiful Carlisle to Settle line. There was a row of four cottages, ours was the second one and was fairly large. It had a large front living room, small kitchen, pantry and three bedrooms, plus the usual outhouses - wash, coal and old style dry toilet. There was no electricity or running water inside the cottage, though there was a water pump situated at the end of the cottages but we were told, that this was not suitable for drinking. Our daily drinking water, however, was delivered every morning and night, seven days a week, from Carlisle Station in four large milk churns, one for each cottage. We had paraffin lights and an old tilley lamp, capable of giving approximately 350 candle power. You had to pump it up. There was a small bottle of methylated spirits on the side and after it got going, you switched it over onto paraffin. All our cooking was done on an old large black range, with an open fire, oven and hobs for pans and kettles. Phyllis soon became adept with it. I guess she had to be with an eight month old baby and a little girl of three!

I remember our very first evening when we couldn't even get the tilley lamp going and had only three candles. I wanted to get some heat into the bedrooms, which all had small black cast iron grates, so I decided to set and light the fires. I soon got one lit, only to find seconds later the room filling with smoke and ash and the fire going out within minutes. I soon discovered that the previous occupants had stuffed a sack up the chimney to stop birds from nesting!

I managed to get this sorted and set off to work on my bicycle to Carlisle for the night shift. When I returned home the following morning, I had to break the ice of the top of the milk churn, in order to get water to boil a kettle for my tea. Minutes later, I had large fires going in both rooms and fixed the tilley lamp. Things were looking up and I went to bed with an easier mind!!

In those early days, bath nights for the girls consisted of a dolly tub in front of the fire, on a handmade peg rug with large fireguard and towels warming by it. They soon got used to this routine and enjoyed their supper afterwards, with bright little faces!

We soon got settled in and I acquired a large allotment alongside the cottage in which we grew a lot of our own produce. I grew all the usual: potatoes, carrots, onions, cabbages and anything else we required.

There were only four cottages, plus the station house but we had our own little community. The Glendinnings lived next door. George was a ganger with the platelayers and had lived there sometime. On the left of us were a young couple with a baby but due to the husband's poor health they had to move into Carlisle.

In the fourth cottage lived, Mavis and Jimmy Sinclair, with their daughter. Jimmy was a railway clerk and they eventually moved to Kirkbride, near Silloth. In the station house itself, we had Peggy and Alf Marshall and he was a shunter at Durran Hill.

Perhaps the ones we came into contact most, was the MacDairmids, when they eventually moved into the house next door. Jean and Johnny moved in with their four children and Johnny was a railway signal and telegraph engineer, at Carlisle. They were both Scottish, Jean from Strathaven, Lanarkshire and Johnny from the Isle of Skye, both with very different accents. They were a lovely family and great to live next door to. I'll never forget the first Hogmanay, as soon as the New Year chimes on the battery powered radio had ended, we heard a knock on the back door and there stood Jean and Johnny, armed with bottles of whisky and other delicacies. What a party we had!

In the summer time we would all go down to the river which wasn't far from the cottages and have picnics. The River Eden was full of salmon at this time and the fishermen got some good catches. Some of the fishermen were elderly and I used to get the job of carrying their catch up the paths to the cars. They would say, "Me being a young fella!"

We were happy and had plenty to keep us occupied. My sister-in-law, Nancy and her husband John used to come from Leicestershire to visit, as did Tom, my late brother-in-law, on his old Royal Enfield motorbike. It took him ten hours I believe! They all loved Cotehill and came as often as they could.

We had a shop, post office, village hall, St John the Baptist Church, school and the Greyhound Pub in Cotehill, which was only two miles away. Mr Joe Killeen had the village shop and when we got our weekly shopping, I used to put the two large holdalls full of groceries on the handlebars of my bike and push it back home. Denise and Nancy both attended primary school there.

Our mail was delivered from Armathwaite Post Office, a village four miles away. The postman cycled and never failed delivering mail, even in winter. He was very kind and thoughtful and used to bring us our supply of 'National Dried Milk' when we required it, which they sold in the Post Office.

Like many others in those days I used to have to cycle to Carlisle, in all weathers. There were two buses a day, three days a week but of course they did not fit in with my shifts. We could not afford a car or motorbike so there was no choice. The worst times, were when you had 'quick shift turn arounds'. I remember setting out on snowy mornings, where you had to dig yourself out and walk pushing your bike for some way before being maybe able to ride it, but no matter what the conditions, you always seemed to make it and never late!

I remember seeing our two daughters, Denise and Nancy, accompanied by our collie dog, 'Bryn', waving eagerly to me, from a stile alongside the Carlisle - Settle line, as I passed on my way to London on the Thames Clyde Express and it used to remind me of the film 'The Railway Children' that we had seen. It was a lovely sight!

Eventually the houses were updated and we got electricity and water. It was a nice community and we enjoyed being part of it, our son, Stephen was born when we were there, on 24 October 1959. Happy times!

Chapter Four
DAYS AT CARLISLE FROM LEADING
PARCEL PORTER TO GUARD

I saw a job advertised for leading parcel porter on the vacany list, applied and got it and was promoted in 1955. We worked three shifts, 6 am - 2 pm, 10 pm - 6 am and 2 pm - 10 pm and always in that order. The worst shift was when you finished at 6 am on a Monday morning and you had to be back on the late shift at 2 pm, they were killers! We would work a twelve week rota, where different jobs were designated to you over these weeks eg 6 am - 2 pm north end, platform 1; 2 -10 pm south end, platform 1; then nights, platform 1. We worked in a link, which was the name given to a group of railwaymen, just as in some jobs people work in particular shifts. There were usually twelve of us in each link, plus we had a parcel foreman and inspector.

Our work used to consist primarily of sorting parcel vans, sorting parcels and mail which would arrive in parcel trains to Carlisle, mostly from the south. These vans arrived three times a day into Carlisle, loaded to the roof with parcels and parcel mail, some of them were so full that if you opened the door the parcels would fall out. Our job was to sort through them because there were parcels to every conceivable destination in Scotland, just loaded on top of one another. We would start by unloading the parcels for Carlisle and then try and make them up for destinations in Scotland. We would for example, make up parcel vans for Dumfries, Kilmarnock and Glasgow and another one for Carstairs, Motherwell and Glasgow. One for Larbert, Stirling and Perth and so on, in other words, if the majority of parcels we found were for Glasgow in one van, we would take all the other parcels out and make that particular van a Glasgow 'proper' as we would call it, and any other for Glasgow out of other vans we would load into that one, and so it went.

I remember Christmas 1958 at Carlisle, I booked on at 6 am on Christmas morning, to find every platform in the station filled with parcel vans loaded up to the roofs with parcels and mails. The reason for this, was quite simply with all the extra trains running for Christmas, it was just impossible for the station to deal with parcel trains until after the Christmas rush was over. With the result, they were all stabled outside the station. Unfortunately, the irony being, we were unloading many parcels which should have been Christmas gifts, but this was often the case in those days.

The railways tried to ease this situation by dealing with at least two parcel trains at Morecambe Promenade Station but I don't think this ever proved successful. I volunteered to go the first year and we were lodged in the railway barracks at

'Black Five' No 45499, north bound on platform 3 at Carlisle Citadel Station, on 12 August 1961 - one of the true workhorses. Note the parcels on platforms 4 and 7. Preston Whiteley Collection

Preston and travelled back and forth to Morecambe every day for six days. It didn't really work for me, or many of the men, being away from home for so long, at this busy time of year.

Another problem we had with these parcel trains was when they were taking the old station roof off Carlisle Citadel Station, also, in 1958. These trains were always dealt with on platform 1 but this was now going to cause problems, so it was decided to deal with these trains at Penrith, on the 'back' platform. This platform was situated away from the normal running of the station. So for a period of three months we were taken to Penrith, in addition to a van load of our own platform barrows, as Penrith had no large barrows to lend us, being only a small station. There we worked on early and late shifts, as a gang of men quite separate from the regular staff at Penrith. The Penrith staff had never seen mail like it before.

As well as the normal daily sorting of parcel vans, we also had to deal with: fish boxes, livestock (calves), tups (rams), baskets of pigeons, coffins (full and empty), boxes of day old chicks and daily newspapers, quite a variety! At this time, eighty per cent of all the parcel traffic we used to handle was mail order and of course literally thousands of mail order catalogues.

Transporting milk at this time was one of the railway's biggest earners. This was either in churns or tanks. One particular firm who used our services, was a dairy company from Appleby, called 'Express Dairy'. A train went from their dairy in Appleby every day conveying tank loads of milk, to Cricklewood in London and thirty or forty empty milk churns would be left daily on flat barrows at the end of one of the platforms, at Carlisle, waiting to be collected and returned to Appleby.

The other big earner then, was racing pigeons, baskets full of them! These were mostly young ones being trained and they would be loaded onto guards vans in baskets, usually thirty or forty baskets, with roughly twenty pigeons in each. These birds came from all over the country. The pigeons requiring releasing at Carlisle, we would take in baskets to the end of the platform to release so they had plenty of room to fly away clear of the station. It was great seeing them take to the sky, with that sudden burst of energy and sense of freedom, the urgency to return as speedily as possible from whence they came! We noted on the tickets attached to the empty baskets the release times and the baskets were then returned to where they had originated from. The young pigeons that were sent locally from Carlisle in early spring, were usually taken to Tebay or Shap to be set off, so they only had a short distance to fly home to start with. These clubs were usually members of the Fur and Feather Society and they were given reduced rail travel rates.

I remember a particular incident from my early days as porter, I was twenty-three or twenty-four years old at the time and it was about 2 am and we were just having a cuppa, when we heard a train arriving at platform 1. I say "heard" because in those days the porter's room was downstairs, underneath the station platform. Well, the door burst open and the duty inspector, Alan Doggart, came running in and went straight over to the elderly porter, Albert Deacon, who we all knew did some part-time work for an undertaker but, of course, we didn't think it had anything to do with that. Alan spoke quietly to Albert, then he immediately jumped to his feet and followed him shouting to me and another young porter, Les Townsend, to follow them which we did although we still didn't have a clue as to what it was all about.

We eventually arrived at the train still following Albert, who had by now entered a coach and gone down the corridor and opened a compartment, with myself and Les, in hot pursuit. Well, all I was able to see over his shoulder was a very old gentleman sitting in the corner seat, with a long pinkish object sticking out of his mouth. It was his tongue, of course! Albert struck this tongue such a blow with his hand, that it shot immediately back into his mouth with the most deafening clunking sound, that I'll never forget!! On seeing this, I ran out of the train as fast as my legs could carry me, bumping into Les and shouting at the same time, "It's a dead body he wants us to help him with!" I could just make out Albert shouting, "Come back you two, he can't hurt you, he's dead!" It didn't matter, we weren't stopping. To rub salt in our wounds or perhaps try to lighten the situation we had found our young selves in earlier, the ticket collector, who was on duty at the ticket barrier approached us and said, "Did anybody remember to collect the gentleman's rail ticket?"

We used to 'fall heir' so to speak, to a variety of different jobs, through people either going off sick or on holiday. Sometimes at the end of a shift, you would maybe be asked if you wanted to do a twelve hour shift for some reason or other, or if they knew in advance, you were just rerostered. The wages I received were very moderate to say the least. I was only on 'bare weeks', which in railway terms meant, no Sundays or rest days worked.

In those days, it was a familiar sight to see van loads of calves being transported in large rail vans, having to travel long distances, mainly to the very far north of Scotland. Carlisle, was one of the places where these loads of calves stopped off, to be 'fed and watered' as they termed it.

Well, one Friday, just after I had started, the roster clerk asked me if I would like to work the following Sunday feeding calves. I had no idea whatsoever what this actually involved but the thought of getting a Sunday, which would pay me time and three quarters, I could not very well say no to. Sunday came and I was there all keen and raring to go at 8 am on the dot. The foreman met me with the words, "Go and find some bottles, any kind will do, beer, lemonade, milk, anything. Then find some rope and make it into loops and also make up six to eight large buckets of powdered milk." There was still at this time, no sign of the calves I was to feed! So with my eight buckets of milk, rope I had made into loops, not forgetting the bottles, I loaded them all onto a platform barrow and proceeded up the platform to one of the bay platforms, where there was now standing three very large vans containing my hungry calves.

There must have been approximately twenty to thirty calves in each van and all running about loose. The procedure which I had been told, was that each calf had to have three bottles of milk and all you had to do was get the neck of the bottle into the side of the mouth. Easier said than done!! When they taste it, I was reliably informed, you would have no trouble giving it the other two and when you had fed one, do not forget to place one of the rope loops round its neck, so you knew which ones had been fed. So with all these instructions, the foreman left me to get started. Well, unfortunately I chose the largest one of the bunch to feed first, my first big mistake. It took the milk with no trouble, so I placed my loop round its neck, proceeded to feed one of the others, only to discover that having tasted the milk, the large one wanted some more and eventually succeeded in upending me with its head between my legs onto the floor amongst the other calves, straw and everything else. Well, you can imagine what I looked and smelled like after feeding eighty to ninety calves. After eight hours and finishing at 4 pm, a little 'worse for wear' to say the least, I can safely say that I never ever volunteered again for a 'spare Sunday' as they termed it, especially feeding calves!

A familiar sight about 10 pm on Sunday nights, was a train from Scotland comprising of six to eight open sided vans, fully enclosed to halfway up, then slatted for ventilation, full of some of the largest cattle, including bulls, I think I have ever seen. These animals were all bound for the cattle dock at Upperby, Carlisle. There, Willie Nelson had the job of feeding, watering and mucking out the vans. I never envied him the job!

Another not very nice job I did at this time, was helping with the fish trains, which travelled daily down from Aberdeen and Fraserburgh. These were quite something in the fifties and more especially so, if you were rostered onto one of the 'rough gangs' as they were called. You worked night shifts and all you did was unload boxes of fish. We used to unload, twenty to thirty vans every night, the majority being wet fish, with quite a number of boxes of kippers in sawdust. These boxes were loaded onto barrows that we wheeled into our large fish house. This was a nightmare in winter, as some of the large boxes used to freeze to the floor of the vans and we used to have to use crowbars to prise them off. This was another of those jobs which had to be done at breakneck speed, as at 4 am the local fish merchants would start arriving to collect their fish from the fish house for distribution to their customers. The fish mongers used to wheel our barrows of fish out to load onto their wagons. After all the fish had gone we hosed down the cement floor of the store so it was ready for the next delivery the following day.

When doing any of these jobs, we always tried to be careful that we did not cut ourselves when handling the fish boxes, as the fish gravy or fluid as it was called, could be a source of infection. In those days we were not supplied with any protective clothing, not even gloves, so you can imagine how we smelt after doing this job and always when I got home, I went straight into the wash house, which was situated outside, to wash and change. This was always nice and warm with the heat from the cast iron boiler, which had been lit the previous night and it also meant we always had hot water on tap.

We also used to dispatch quite a large consignment of sausages by rail from Cavaghan & Gray, a local Carlisle firm. There was one particular small box, which was sent to a small place called Helmsdale, in the very north of Scotland. There was only the one train, the 'Royal Highlander', that went from London Euston to Inverness and it left Carlisle at 1.30 am. It was always the standing joke, "Have the sausages for Helmsdale gone?" I don't think they ever missed that train. I often wondered who that butcher was in Helmsdale?

Daily newspapers were another daily chore and came in large heavy bundles, with the string cutting into your fingers. We unloaded roughly eighty to a hundred bundles every night, all at breakneck speed, as Menzies, the people who collected them from us, were always working to a tight schedule, as these papers obviously had to be out first thing to their customers. Obviously, we were never popular if the train was late.

One night though, we opened a van to unload some newspapers, only to find that six young greyhounds had had great fun chewing through a bundle, which now resembled confetti and had to be swept out. The greyhounds had obviously not been tied up sufficiently far enough away and had kept themselves busy during their long eight hour journey from London and, of course, unknown to the poor guard! In those days dogs travelling unaccompanied were always taken off the train at various places enroute for the toilet and exercise and it was all part of the rail service. If you ever saw a dog running along the platform, it was a standard joke, "Stop that dog, it's a parcel!" Sometimes, of course, it wasn't a joke, it may well have been travelling on the guards van and had made good its escape with label flapping round its neck, with its desired destination thereon. Fortunately the occurrence of loosing animals enroute didn't happen often and now, of course, this does not happen, as pets do not travel unaccompanied.

Jimmy Leslie was the last station master at Carlisle before the railways were nationalised in 1948 but still continued working in that position afterwards. Mr Leslie was quite a strict disciplinarian. I remember on one occasion, I was working the 'Thames Clyde Express' and I was standing on the platform waiting for it to come in, with my uniform all pressed and smart looking. I had taken the wire out of my cap, so I could pin the sides down. I thought it looked better that way! Mr Leslie wasn't at all suited and came up and asked me what train I was working and I told him. He then said, "Not with a cap like that on, you look like a captain off one of these American tramp steamers! Get it changed immediately." I did as well!

The first railway strike I remember was in 1955. I forget how long this lasted but it was an ASLEF strike, which involved drivers and firemen in those days, because we still had steam then. I remember the station announcer saying over his tannoy, "The train standing on platform No1, might be leaving at so and so time, providing a driver and fireman turn up and if they happen to be members of the NUR Union, you will be in luck!" Some of the loco men were in the NUR and they were not involved in the dispute but the atmosphere was often very tense in these disputes because the ASLEF members fully expected their support. I have known best of mates to fall out for life over disputes like this, his mate being an ASLEF member and the other in the NUR. Years later when I worked at Oxenholme we had weeks of one and two day strikes for ASLEF drivers but the longer they went on, the more the passengers began to treat them 'as a way of life' and adapt accordingly.

Christmas in those days was just an ordinary working day and whilst portering at Carlisle, I was required to work every Christmas but I must say I was luckier than some, I was always fortunate enough to get the early shift, so I was home for dinner with the family.

I also worked in the left luggage office at Carlisle, this was usually to fill in for illness and holidays. The summer months were busy, especially so during Glasgow Fair fortnight, when all the tradesmen went on holiday. It was not unusual to take anything between £40 - £50 in an hour and this was when it was sixpence (two and half pence) a case and many's the time they were deposited for less than an hour. So you can imagine we were quite busy!

We used to get tips from passengers for carrying their luggage, this was before passenger luggage trolleys (pre 1970's), were even thought of, let alone invented! Some of the porters would think up all sorts of ways to boost up a tip, if they thought they had a chance. One particular instant that springs to mind, when a particular porter was instructed to help an American tourist and his wife on a train. Well, before the train arrived, they asked the porter if it was possible for him to get them a first class compartment to themselves, to which the porter assured them it would be no problem whatsoever. So when the train arrived, our porter with this request in mind, noticed where the first class accommodation was situated, even before the train had come to a stop but immediately proceeded to go the opposite direction altogether. He went up the platform running very quickly, with our American couple a long way behind. He then ran into a room, where he knew there was a cold water tap and proceeded to dowse his head under it, with the result when he came out he just resembled someone wringing with sweat. Well, he eventually arrived at some more first class compartments with the Americans in hot pursuit and when they saw him, they were heard to say, "My look at the sweat on you, you needn't have put yourself to all that trouble on our behalf!" To which our intrepid porter replied, "We always try to oblige!" Noticing also, that they had increased his tip from 2/6 to 5/- (12 ½p to 25p), which was double, and a fairly large tip in those days. Little did they know of course, that when the train arrived in the first instance, the first class accommodation was directly opposite to where they were standing but to our porter friend, this would have been much too easy and only worth 2/6, not 5/-, with which he was rewarded, for all the trouble he had gone to! If they had only known!

Another story I remember and this time involved 'The Caledonian'. Now this train ran from Glasgow to London and its first stop was London for passengers. This meant that it ran straight through, bar changing the engine at Crewe. Well another of our porters was once again being very attentive. Again, he had some Americans to assist on the train, but this time, with an enormous amount of luggage as well. Now this particular train was only scheduled to stop for two minutes at the platform and our porter was well aware of this but still insisted in putting all the luggage on the racks. With the result, the door was slammed shut from the outside and the train moved off with our ever helpful porter still on board. Now this was 10.20 am and at 4 pm, a phone call was received to inform us, that the porter had arrived at Euston and could someone tell his wife where he was. He got his leg pulled for weeks afterwards. It's one thing putting cases on for passengers but to go three hundred miles to take them off, was taking things a little bit too far to say the least! Though to be true, he did get the last laugh and was paid up until the time he arrived back in Carlisle at 9 pm - quite a day!

My twin brother, Bill, also used to work in the station and quite often people thought they were seeing double. One instance, was when I was working in the left luggage office and my brother used to call in to have a chat with me on his lunch break, when I was on the early shift. Well this particular day, an old porter,

Class 3F 0-6-0 No 47471 at Carlisle on 21 August 1963.
That's just like the one that came of the rails!   *Preston Whiteley Collection*

Caledonian 'Class 7' No.
46234, at platform 4
Carlisle Citadel Station,
going south - the cream
of loco's for passenger
work only.

Preston Whiteley
Collection

whom I always got along with quite well, asked me if he could leave his new supply of uniform with me and he would collect it the next day. I quickly agreed saying, "Of course, no problem, I'll put it in the back for you." I forgot to tell him I was on rest day the following day and my relief would be there in my place, when the old porter came for his uniform. Unfortunately, my brother was standing at the window chatting to the relief and this is when the trouble started. I had put his uniform away safely but between them they were unable to find it. The old porter's patience was beginning to wain as he turned to my brother, obviously thinking it was me, saying "Where did you put my uniform?" To which my brother replied, "He hadn't a clue, as he didn't work here." At this the poor old porter walked off, minus his new uniform and just a little annoyed, as you can imagine. When I returned to work he practically ignored me. I ventured to ask him if he had got the uniform alright and of course the penny dropped and I discovered the mix-up that had occurred. I explained it must have been my twin brother to which he replied, "Pull the other one, it has bells on!" He didn't know I had a twin but nevertheless didn't speak to me ever again.

A lot of the amusing things seemed to happen on nights and this is a sort of joke that someone played on me while I was working in left luggage. Standing outside on the platform was a high-sided four wheeled barrow, with a rope netting over it, obviously livestock of some sort, waiting to go on a train. I was very busy at the time with people depositing luggage etc, so I did not get the chance to have a look in it for myself. Then a guard passed by the window and I saw him looking in the barrow very hesitantly and he shouted, "Be careful, John, there's a young lion in there!" Well, of course, I just laughed it off, knowing full well he must be joking. Well after a while, things began to quieten down in the left luggage office and curiosity was getting the better of me, so I sneaked out to have a look in the barrow, only to find it was a lovely young pony. What made it worse, was that the guard who had pulled the joke on me was now leaning out of the window of the passing train, with a big smile on his face and shouted to me, "Funny old lion that, John!" I really fell for that one!

I remember an incident which involved boxes full of 'live' lobsters, which we had to unload from the guards van of a train. Well this should normally have been a straight forward task but one of the boxes had got accidentally broken open, with the result, all these lobsters were now crawling about the van floor and none of us obviously fancied the job of lifting them up with our hands and putting them back into the repaired box. So we went for a brush and shovel and put them back in this way. What we failed to notice was that some had strayed up the corridor of the coach and were now making their way very swiftly into the first compartment, which was full of middle aged ladies! Well, it was the screams and yells which drew our attention and when we got to their compartment, we found them all trying to stand out of the way of our lobsters, on the seats and some were even trying to scramble on the luggage racks! We apologised to them all and retrieved our lobsters as quickly as possible by brush and shovel!

During the late fifties a couple of the lads had a thriving business going, collecting all the empty beer and lemonade bottles which were left in the trains. They used to do this when they were engaged in cleaning the carriages while they were in the sheds. Then they would return them to the local breweries and collect the deposits on them. Quite lucrative at the time!

After a while I noticed a vacancy come up for a shunter at Carlisle, so I thought I would apply for it. I enjoyed all the jobs I had done but the more experience you got, the more chance you had in promotion in the railways, just like any other job. Anyway, I was lucky and once again got it and did it for six months. Shunting is just the moving of vehicles, detaching and attaching vehicles to and from trains, making parcel trains up of parcel vans and putting milk tanks on the rear of trains and such like. This was all done in sidings and platforms at Carlisle Station and I learned from a fine bunch of chaps. I remember the first vacuum pipes I had to connect together, I think I did everything but stand on my head and my arms ached terribly. Luckily, I was not holding a train up, as I was just practising in a siding but I soon got the knack after a few cuts and bruises. There was a set procedure you had to keep to and this was for your own safety as well. Firstly there was the coupling, then the steam pipes, lighting cables and lastly the vacuum pipes. It was common sense really because if you did connect the vacuum first, then the train could possibly move off with you still in between the coaches. The firemen always used to uncouple their own engine.

It really was quite a hard, rough sort of job shunting in these days, especially on nights, if you were working with the shunting engine called, the 'lankey pilot', this was the term used for the little lightweight 3F's engines which were used to attach and detach vans. You never stopped working all night and of course were out in all weathers. I remember one shunter I worked with, Nelson Hart, had so much oil on the back of his jacket he never needed to wear a raincoat, the rain just rolled of it, like water off a duck's back!

In this particular job, you always had an appreciative audience, if not an anxious one, owing to the possibility of accidentally getting trapped between the buffers. Doesn't bear thinking about! Seriously, it was and still is a very dangerous job and you cannot afford to be unaware of what you are about and even today, other than the coupling, it still requires a person to get between the engine or coaches to connect the air pipes.

I remember one early morning about 4 am, when I was working at Carlisle

B.R. 8714/

BRITISH RAILWAYS..**REGION.**   Vac. No.............................

List No. ....

VACANCY FOR...

at... Class............................

To.. Date...............................19........

I desire to apply for the above-mentioned vacancy and have satisfied myself that the post would be suitable to me in every respect.

(If the application is for a Salaried staff vacancy, experience or special qualifications to be shown overleaf, using the top half of the form).

Name (in block letters)...

Grade and Class... Department..

Station..

Signature..

FOR OFFICE USE

Age or date of birth	Service in each step of promotion diagram					
	Step 1	Step 2	Step 3	Step 4	Step 5	Step 6

ACKNOWLEDGMENT

*Application received for vacancy No...................................List No..............................

Signed..Date..............................19........

*To Name ....

Grade ....

Station ....

* To be completed by applicant.

Vacancy forms - I filled in quite a few of these during the years!

Station, as a shunter in 1958 and we were sitting in the cabin having a cup of tea, when the fireman of the shunt engine, which was a Class 3F, came running in to tell us 'they had come off the road', which in laymen's terms, meant the engine had fallen off the rails. Well, we all started to panic, all except Arthur Gledhill, our yard foreman who had been a good friend of my father's. He was a bit on the stout side and had a very commanding figure and voice to match. I remember his words to this day, "Come on all of you!" Well, we all followed him to where the engine was standing with just the two rear wheels off and fortunately it was in a back siding, which was not always used. Arthur immediately took charge of the situation, he told us to get some old wooden sleepers, which were lying nearby and start chocking them under the wheels. After that he shouted to the driver to reverse the engine very slowly. We all crossed our fingers and held our breath and to our great amazement, this seventy-five ton engine dropped very quietly back onto the rails. Then Arthur just shouted, "Right lads, back in the cabin, back to normal!" What a relief!

Today, I suppose had it happened, it would have involved the use of steam cranes and gangs of men being called in especially to deal with it. Whereas then, there were about six of us including the fireman, under the expert guidance of Arthur, an experienced railwayman. I rather suspect though, that he had maybe dealt with a similar situation in the past, nevertheless, he was one of that breed of railwaymen who made light work of major problems.

I was told the story about a shunter and a driver from away. One night the driver was sitting in the shunter's cabin and the shunter came in carrying his shunter's pole under his arm and the driver said to him jokingly, "I bet you could knock someone out with that, if you didn't like them!" With no further ado the shunter said, "Don't bet on such a thing!" and hit the driver one almighty bang on his head, knocking him out cold. With the result he finished up in hospital in Preston, with severe concussion for three days. The shunter obviously didn't have a sense of humour!

In 1960 I applied for a guard's position, I was put through the standard test, regarding all the rules and regulations appertaining to the running of trains and after successfully passing the test, I had to learn 'the road' and this was done working alongside an experienced guard. In otherwords, it meant you had to know every signal box, sidings, catch points, where situated, gradients, tunnels and of course every station on the line you were going to work on. This could take up to three months to learn and then you were finally passed out on all parcels, mails, livestock, newspapers, etc, you had in your van. The one duty you were not responsible for in those days, was the issuing and examining of tickets.

The issuing was done at all stations, there were no unstaffed stations then and the examining was done by a travelling ticket collector, work which my father had done. You also had journals to keep up-to-date, everything had to be recorded on them, engine number, driver's name, where he came from, all the carriage numbers, weights, times at stations, even the weather and any other relevant information, including delays and the reason for them. I suppose, it could be compared to a ship captain's log and these journals had to be kept up-to-date between the different points on the route. For example, if you worked a train from Carlisle to London St Pancras, you had one to make out between, Carlisle and Skipton, then Skipton and Leeds, and so on - Leeds to Sheffield, Sheffield to Leicester, Leicester to Kettering and the last, was between Kettering and St Pancras. Quite a job in those days but compared to what is required of a guard these days, issuing and examining of tickets, arrival announcements for stations, I think I preferred the old days. You were not involved so much with the passengers then, we were more concerned with the operational side of the job. A basic guard on top link wage, received £9.5s per week in the 1960's. This was a guard who made long distance journeys, like myself.

During the time I was 'learning the road' to Glasgow Central, we had the job of taking our empty coaches to the carriage sheds at Bellahouston, in Glasgow and then we had to walk back to Glasgow Central. This was at 10 o'clock on a Saturday night and we had to walk right through the Gorbals district of Glasgow, which had a terrible reputation then of being notoriously rough, to say the least. I remember the guard I was with warning me in no uncertain terms that you had to be ready for anything being thrown over the railway fence, from bottles, chairs, bedsteads, you name it. It was quite frightening really and this was what you got with walking on the railway line. Of course we were supposed to walk back by the road for our own safety but no chance! All things considered we always thought it was safer walking on the railway line.

I remember the first train I ever worked, it was the 'Thames Clyde Express' from Carlisle to Skipton. It was on a Sunday and I can honestly say it was one of the most nerve racking experiences I think I ever went through, so much so, on leaving Carlisle I forgot to close my van door. Luckily for me it was an in-swinging door and it was brought to my attention by the ticket collector, who came into the van saying, "It would be a good idea if you close your door, son!"

I always had a great respect for sleeping car attendants. I remember once working a train through the night not long after I had started as a guard and not being sure of the road during daylight, let alone in darkness. It was a terrible night, pouring with rain, when we came to a stand somewhere out in the wilds and I have to admit, I hadn't a clue where I was. Well, after we had stood for about five minutes, I was beginning to panic, when my van door opened which led into the first sleeping car. In calmly walked the sleeping car attendant, Bill

The 'Thames Clyde Express' approaching our house on its way to London St Pancras on 29 April 1956.
This was the first train I worked on as guard.   Robert Leslie

Crooks. He reassured me, saying it was nothing to worry about, we were at such and such a place and "they do occasionally stop here and we would be on our way shortly," at which point we moved off. I could not thank him enough, to which he turned and said, "If I can't help old Dick Cottam's son, it's a bad job!" It turned out that my father and he had travelled this route together for quite a lot of years, so he was keeping a friendly eye on me.

On long journeys such as up to London, we used to stop over at railway barracks, just as my father had. I slept at Kentish Town, Willesden, Camden, all in London. I also stayed at Crewe, Cresty Road and Preston. The barracks were to be found all over the country, just as in my father's day. We always slept through the day when we were in London particularly, the conditions in some used to leave a lot to be desired but I must say Kentish Town Hostel was always very quiet through the day.

Protection of your train, was an important role, also covered by a guard and had to be performed if your train was derailed or broken down. You were expected to walk back from the rear of your train and place a detonator. The detonator was a small round disc, about an inch or so in diameter, with two pieces of plastic to attach to the flange of the rail. These were put on the rail at a ¼ mile, another one at ½ mile and three detonators three yards apart at ¾ mile and remain there displaying a red flag by day and a red light at night. If a tunnel intervened you had to put three detonators at the mouth of the tunnel, proceed through the tunnel and place a further three when you came out of the tunnel. If by any chance you arrived at a signal box, you had to put three detonators outside the box and go into the box and explain to the signalman what had happened to your train.

I myself performed these duties twice, in all the time I was a guard. The first one was between Gargrave and Hellifield and the second time was between Bingley and Shipley. Both times was engine failure on Diesel Motor Units (DMUs).

I remember my father telling me about the time he was involved in a derailment when he was a guard. This was at Kettering in the early fifties, I think. It concerned the train he was working from London and it ran into the rear of a goods train. I remember seeing a photograph of his Engine No 5581, lying on its side in a cornfield. He said he had known nothing until he felt this almighty bump and then he noticed the vacuum gauge in his van plummet to zero and the next thing was all these crates of apples in the van came down on top of him and feeling concussed and shaken. He nevertheless, managed to climb out of his van and carried out his duty, following his training re protection of his train and walking a distance of ¾ a mile. He was complimented for his actions by the Chairman of the Inquiry he attended a few months afterwards. Coincidentally, one day when I was performing guard duty and I was working the 08.05 am, a local stopping train to Hellifield and my engine that day was none other than the 5581. When I told my father about it, he said he would have been very reluctant to travel ever again behind that particular engine!

Another rule we had to carry out in those days was Rule 55. This rule came into being should your train come to a stand at a signal which did not have a diamond on the signal post. The driver had to go immediately to the signal box, to sign the signalman's book and after doing that, he had to make sure the signalman put a collar on the signal lever, thereby protecting his train, preventing him from pulling the signal off while his train was standing still. Of course these days, these rules are hardly ever called upon, as every signal has a telephone on it and with power boxes the signalman knows immediately where every train is on a particular part of the line.

In the 1950's, you could quite often seen a full circus travelling by train. I remember I came to work one night at Carlisle, starting work as usual at 10 pm and standing on the platform was a train full of animals, which formed part of a circus. One van I noticed in particular, was rocking from side to side and looked as if at any moment it would topple over. On looking inside, I saw four young elephants, two each end of the van and resting on a make shift bed on the floor in the middle, was a young chap. On seeing me he jumped to his feet and asked very politely if I could get him some cigarettes from out of the refreshment room, which was directly opposite to where the van was standing. He said, he hoped I didn't mind him asking, he would have gone himself, the only problem being that the elephants would insist on coming too!! So needless to say, I went for his cigarettes with the greatest of pleasure!

Another night when I was working 10 pm (or 22.00 hours as we used to call it by the 24 hr clock), out of Edinburgh Waverley to London St Pancras train. Loaded in my van were quite a large number of rare birds in boxes, eagles etc enroute to some show in the Midlands. The people who owned them were all travelling with them and when we got under way from Edinburgh, I thought I would have a quick glance into some of the boxes. The first couple I looked at contained cages within the boxes and these were canaries, I think and some other small foreign birds. Curiosity began to get the better of me and I was anxious to see what was in the larger box and I very soon found out. On opening it, a very large bird flew out into the van and perched itself on top of a pile of mail bags. I started to panic, the main thing I suppose was it being night time, luckily there were no windows open but by this time we were fast approaching our first station stop and I knew I would be getting some mail in, which would involve more than one door at least being opened.

So, when I heard the brakes being applied, I very quickly sneaked through the adjoining door into the coach immediately in front of my van and on arriving at the platform, stuck my head out and yelled in a very loud voice to my colleagues on the platform, not to open any of the doors of my van. I explained the reason to them and would they help me to retrieve the bird, which they did with great difficulty and to my relief. I have forgotten now how I explained the delay to the train but I can safely say, I never ever looked in boxes containing birds, ever again!

One of the best things about my job was the interesting people I met both in the job and travelling by rail. I remember an old signalman. I was on my way to London with the overnight train as the guard, when for some reason I cannot remember now, we were stopped by signals at Mallerstang signal box. Now this box was really out in the wilds, miles from anywhere. I climbed down from my guards van and mounted the three or four steps to the door which was locked. On seeing me the old signalman came and unlocked it and let me in and before he could warn me, I slipped the full length of his floor which was shining like glass. You were supposed to step onto two cloths as you walked in, everything in that signal box was spotless, big blazing fire burning up the chimney but what I remember mostly about that visit, was the old chap asking me where I was going with the train. I said, "To London of course!" He then repeated the name London slowly and confessed that any large city would scare the life out of him and told me that he had never in his life been any further than Appleby, which was less than twenty miles away from where he worked and he didn't desire to either! He must have been a chap nearing retirement and had worked in that same signal box all his working life. I guess there were many like him in those days and very dedicated men they were.

The Queen came to Carlisle in the Royal Train to attend a Railway Exhibition but was unable to leave the train, as she was suffering from sinus trouble. So the decision was taken for the Duke of Edinburgh to attend the ceremony on his own and for the Queen to be taken immediately back to London by train. This was not quite so straight forward as it would first seem and created quite a few rail problems. Firstly, the train was not originally supposed to depart until 4 pm and the time now was only 10 am. Secondly, the guard who was booked to work it to London was not due to book on until 3 pm. So arrangements had to be made to send out at all speed for this guard, with an urgent request for him to book on as soon as possible.

They sent a messenger called, Alf 'Piggy' Wilkinson, who went round in his pig wagon of all things, with the swill bins rattling in the back. This being the middle of summer, the off duty guard was found busy cutting his privet hedge. Yes, he would come as soon as he could, but not before he had finished what he was doing. He had no intention whatsoever in leaving it unfinished, 'not even for the Queen of England'! I suppose he could not have spoken truer words. Regardless of what he said, he did make a special effort and the Queen was on her way in good time. He did, however, tell us though, that the Queen had apologised to him for being such a nuisance!

The railway had of course certain set procedures regarding the Royal Train. One being that whenever the train arrived at Carlisle enroute to Scotland, the Scottish Region, required that the engine had to be replaced by two shining 'Black Fives', regardless of time, day or night. 'Black Fives' were marvellous engines, they were shining black as their name denotes and were real work horses being used for freight and passengers. To railway people the Royal Train was always referred to as 'The Grove', this being the full train itself. Sometimes if the Queen herself was not travelling and maybe only one member of the Royal Family was on board and they did not require the full train but maybe just a few Royal coaches, then these would be coupled to a normal train and that train would then be referred to as a 'Deepdene Special'.

The Northern Irishman was the name given to the boat train that ran between London Euston and Stranraer Harbour, for Larne sailings and ran via Castle Douglas until 1965. This train departed Carlisle at 1.20 am to Euston but on some occasions if it happened to run late, it would coincide with the opposite one going to Stranraer Harbour. When this occurred, it meant that the one to Euston was standing on platform No 3 and the one to Stranraer was on platform No 1 and in between these two platforms, was the refreshment room. In those days, these trains each had boards on the side of the coaches stating where the train had come from and where it was going eg the train to Euston would have, "Northern Irishman - Stranraer Harbour to London Euston," and the other train would have the same but vice-versa.

You will have no doubt have guessed what used to occur. You would get our friendly Irishman, getting off the Euston train and quickly entering the refreshment room for some more 'liquid refreshment' coming off platform No 3 in a slightly inebriated state. Then when the trains sets to go, he would quickly leave mistakenly by the other door leading onto platform No 1 and then seeing the name Stranraer on the side, would join the wrong train and get on the one going back to Stranraer. They usually made it to about Dumfries before they realised they were going back to where they had just come from. This needless to say also applied to some of the passengers travelling the other way and they usually got as far as Preston before they realised their error. This was always a problem with these two trains. I suppose on reflection we were as confused as they were at times and when an Irishman has had a few bevvies too many, he is not the easiest of persons to understand or to ascertain whether he is coming or

Shining 'Black Five' No 45348 at Carlisle, standing on the middle line between platforms 3 and 4. 'Black Fives' were put on the Royal Trains when they travelled north of Carlisle. Photo taken 12 August 1960.   Preston Whiteley Collection

'Flying Scotsman' in Carnforth Shed on 2 April 1966. I count myself very lucky to have been guard on the Waverley Express and being pulled by this engine, a gleeming green A3 Pacific - one of the greatest engines!   *Preston Whiteley Collection*

going. Sometimes we thought we were even maybe guilty of directing them onto the wrong train or were we just getting a bit paranoid about it all! I've even seen a person sitting on one train when I knew fine well they should have been on the other one and on telling them this fact, they were even more reluctant to move, fully convinced they were on the right train. I was almost tempted to stand in the middle of the refreshment room with two placards, one on each hand, saying, 'London' and the other one 'Stranraer'!

I count myself lucky to have been a guard on the 'Waverley Express' which ran between London St Pancras and Edinburgh Waverley via the North British route from Carlisle and I remember being pulled by one of the greatest engines of all time, 'The Flying Scotsman', a gleaming green A3 Pacific. I was also fortunate to have worked the famous 'Thames Clyde Express', which used to run between London St Pancras and Glasgow St Enoch, (which has also gone), pulled by the 'Royal Scot' Class 6 engines, nearly all belonging to the Holbecks Shed, in Leeds. These engines used to work from there to Glasgow and London. In those days you always got a fresh engine on at Leeds City North Station, today that station is a parcel concentration depot. In the late fifties/early sixties it was a brand new station, with a lovely large concourse, with chandeliers and a cinema. Sadly today, that concourse is the car park for Leeds Central Station. In the past the Leeds City North Station was the Midland Railway Station and the Central was always referred to as, the North Eastern Railway Station.

There was a train I christened, the 'Medicine Train', it was actually the 1.28 pm from Carlisle to Edinburgh Waverley. This train used the Waverley Line by the North British route via Hawick, St Boswells and Galashiels to Edinburgh, but these were the principal stations. I was more concerned with the little out of the way stations, such as Riddings Junction, Penton, Kershopefoot, Steele Road and so on. Now this particular train I believe was the only one that called at all these stations. The reason I called it this, was because when I boarded my van at Carlisle, I noticed all these different prescriptions, pills, medicines, potions etc, all lined up in station order on my desk. I inquired what these were in aid of, only to be told they would all be collected from me in due course when I arrived at these small places and so it was. Young mothers, elderly men and women would come along to my van and ask, "Do I have so and so for Mrs Jones and so on and cough mixture for her little boy, Johnny?" I suppose in those days, the train was the only means of getting these supplies to them. The amazing thing was, I never ever saw who actually brought the medicine to the train at Carlisle but I always felt that I had helped out in some little way in providing that invaluable service.

I do remember though in particular, a station on that same line, Riccarton Junction, it was called and it had its own Co-Operative shop on the platform and

The 'Sansovino' No 60053 at Hawick on 29 July 1960, on the Waverley Line is similar to the train I called the 'Medicine Train' that travelled at this time.   *Preston Whiteley Collection*

one got the feeling that the whole place depended on the train for everything. Time has moved on, of course, and that line like a lot of others, has closed and has been for many years though there are always inklings of trying to reopen some.

Usually at Christmas, as I said, I was fortunate in getting an early shift so I could be home with the family for dinner. One Christmas, however, I had to work the 'Thames Clyde Express' as far as Skipton. A few weeks before, I was asked if I would like my Christmas lunch on the train, naturally I accepted. So off to work I went, telling Phyllis not to bother with any dinner for me. After leaving Carlisle, I fully expected to be called to take my lunch almost immediately as I was only working the train the short distance to Skipton. Instead, I was only called to the dining car after leaving Hellifield, which left me approximately 10-15 minutes to eat my dinner and I only just managed my soup. So that was my Christmas dinner for that year! Unfortunately for me, the dining car staff were obviously under the impression I was working the train to London, still never mind, the food would taste all the better when I got home.

Chapter Five
CROSSING KEEPER, BURNESIDE
(1961-65)

I first heard of a small village called Burneside early in 1961, when I saw a notice in our Time Office, at Carlisle. It was advertising at this time positions for a male and female crossing keeper, at Higher Crossing, Burneside, near Kendal. Included in the offer was the cottage attached to the crossing, comprising of living room, kitchen, two bedrooms and fitted bathroom. I made a quick mental note of the details, so I could discuss it later with Phyllis, to see what she said. Her first words were, "Burneside, where's that?" Anyway after explaining everything and talking it over we decided it looked promising and applied for it, even though in doing so, it would mean a down grade from my present job as guard, to that of crossing keeper but we thought it would be worth it. It would mean 'living on the job' so to speak, no more cycling twenty miles a day, in all weathers but nevertheless, we would be sorry to say goodbye to Cotehill, where we had spent many happy times.

We were successful and moved to Burneside on a warm sunny day on 12 May 1961, to become the new crossing keepers. Burneside is situated just two miles out of Kendal and has the large James Croppers paper mill, that employs many of the locals and produces high quality paper which is exported all over the world. The Cropper family live at Tolston Hall, which is just on the outskirts of the village. The village originally had a Mill School for the local children and it was said, when the coal hopper trains used to trundle past full of coal, lessons had to be halted as the noise was deafening! Later in 1964 a new primary school was built, together with a new council estate.

The vicar of St Oswalds Church then, was the Reverend Norman Casson, the village postmaster was Bill Peill, publican of the Jolly Anglers Pub was Dick Clarke, a genial host. The manager of the local Co-Operative store at this time was Billy Martin, an ex-Japanese POW and the village bakery was run by John Bowness and his wife. So we had all the facilities we needed in close proximity and we soon became part of the community.

As my wife, Phyllis, was taking the job of the other crossing keeper, she was required to learn all the rules and regulations appertaining to it, plus learning how to pull the correct levers for the signals. Quite a challenge! Which I am happy to say, Phyllis rose to with no problem and passed with flying colours! She became quite a favourite with all the drivers and firemen passing through the crossing.

Higher Crossing cottage, Burneside, where we lived from 1961-68
and the railway line is on the right.

The crossing gates at Higher Crossing, Burneside - the original heavy wooden ones.
Note the two paraffin lamps on the gates.

The crossing cabin at Higher Crossing, Burneside, where I spent a lot of time.

Stephen my son at the cottage door at Higher Crossing, Burneside, aged two years old.

In these days Burneside was a thriving station. Raymond Dixon was the station master and Ted Sharpe was the porter/signalman. The station consisted of two platforms, an up and a down, a signal box and two goods sidings. Two freight trains called morning and late afternoon, five days a week. We had also approximately twenty passenger trains a day, all still steam hauled, on this busy little branch line. During the busy summer months, we had weekend extras, which were excursion trains coming to Windermere from all parts of the country.

The crossing was manned from 5 am to 11 pm or sometimes later at night if a train was a bit late. One of us would do the 5 am - 1pm shift and the other the 3 pm - 11 pm. I, as the resident crossing keeper, always did the extra two hours at dinner time. Phyllis got paid £6.15 shillings and I was paid £7.15 shillings. This meant of course, we were never able to go out together, as one of us had always to be in attendance but we worked it to suit ourselves. If, for instance, one of the children was ill and Phyllis was unable to do her duty, I would be able to step in and do both tours. Fortunately, our bosses did not mind as long as one of us was there. Again, as the resident crossing keeper I was sometimes expected to do extra hours but was never paid overtime for this. We worked seven days a week and the only time off we had together was our fortnight's holiday which had to be taken each year between April and September and they put two relief men on to cover for this. We bought our first car when we were there, it was a black Hillman Minx with the column gear change. We had our own transport at last.

The crossing opened every morning at 5 o'clock when we started duty. We had to ring the signalman at Oxenholme to inform him that the crossing was open and if you omitted to do this he would have to caution the driver on the first train, informing him to be prepared to stop at the signal protecting the crossing and ascertain what the trouble was. I think we overslept three times during the six years we were there and it was embarrassing to say the least, for we would be awakened by a very loud whistle from the steam engine or the loud knocking at the front door of our cottage by the fireman. Fortunately, we were never reported and we were quickly in business and had the problem rectified within a few minutes, so we were lucky! Our neighbours used to tease us saying "Slept in again this morning we heard!"

The crossing cabin at Burneside was equipped with a railway telephone, an internal phone in other words, which was connected to the other level crossings on the Windermere line, namely the Lower Crossing at Burneside (ours being Higher Crossing) and Staveley Crossing and all the signal boxes and stations on the line including Oxenholme. It also had a coal stove, table and easy chair and for lighting it had a large paraffin lamp hanging down from the roof, all very cosy. The main item was the two block instruments, one for the up line and one for the down line. The up line being the one from Windermere to Oxenholme and the down one from Oxenholme to Windermere, in other words simply to tell us when a train was coming.

These instruments were like two dials (as shown) with a pointer and three sections. When the pointer was straight up it read 'line clear', when it was to the left it read 'train approaching' and when it was turned to the right it read 'train on line'. These instruments were worked electronically by the signalman each side of the crossing, namely Windermere and Kendal.

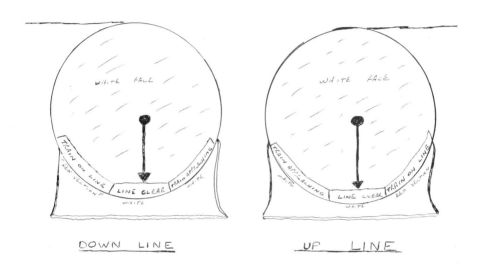

Two block instruments. These were worked electronically by the signalmen each side of the crossing, namely Windermere and Kendal.

Thus, when a train was approaching Kendal the signalman there would turn our dial to 'train approaching' and when it left Kendal, he would turn our dial to 'train on line' and this would be a signal to us to close our gates to the road and pull our signal off immediately. The dial would remain in the 'train on line' position until the train had arrived at Windermere, where the signalman there would then move our dial to 'line clear'. Particular attention had to be paid to these instruments especially when you knew there was another train due. You had to watch for the dial to go to the 'line clear' position and in turn watch for it going immediately to the 'train approaching' position and then to 'train on line' signifying that another train had left Kendal.

On the down line it was much the same procedure, when a train was ready to leave Windermere the signalman there would place our up dial, to 'train approaching' and when it left it would go to 'train on line'. There was not the same urgency to close the gates because we had at least twenty minutes before the train was due to pass us and when it did eventually arrive at Kendal, our dial would go back to 'line clear' signifying again that the line was clear for another train to leave Windermere.

All this might seem quite complicated to the layman but to us it became a way of life. From the safety aspect it simply meant that a train could not leave Kendal until the previous train had arrived at Windermere. In railway terms, as we used to put it, 'until it was 'knocked' out of section'.

Other times when you had to be very alert on the job, were during the very busy periods, summer time especially. This was when Burneside and Staveley signal boxes were required to open, 'to split the section up', as it was termed, meaning quite simply to speed the trains up to and from Windermere.

We also used to ring Staveley Crossing by phone, when a train had left Burneside and they would do the same when their train left Staveley. It was just an added safety measure though the practice was not always favoured by management.

Working at the crossing could have its down side, that being adverse weather conditions. During the winter months we had, gales, rain, snow and ice, not forgetting the fog at Burneside.

I am sure we would not have been so conscious of the elements if we hadn't become so involved in the open air aspects. The gales could be very severe and trying to open the heavy wooden gates became a battle to get them into their position, particularly for my wife who is small in stature and if the rain decided to join in, you were soaked to the skin despite protective clothing. I used to scuttle into the warm and cosy cabin, whilst being warmed up by the coal stove waiting for the train to pass, steam was coming from my wet clothes (a case of 'rising damp' I think!), when the train did pass it was out on the crossing again to open the gates for the road traffic to go over. I was never dry until the last engine left Windermere and passed us, then we could close up for the night.

Snow and ice were an additional problem, the signal levers which were in an open ground frame alongside the cabin, used to freeze solid after a heavy overnight frost. When I got up at 5 am next morning, all I could do was to chip away the ice at the base of the levers and when I had done that, I used to get a hot cloth and place it on the lever handle lock, to thaw the ice enough to enable me to pull both the distant and home signals, to the 'off' position. I might add by this stage my fingers were as frozen as the levers.

With snow, if there was a heavy fall overnight and it had drifted on the gates, it prevented us from opening them to let a train through. So at 5 am you had to work frantically to dig and sweep the snow away from the gates and off the crossing itself. I must say, it always warmed you up, if only by the thought of holding the train up!

Fog was always very eerie to work in, with visibility practically nil and sounds were muffled. You really had to have your wits about you once the indicators on the block switched to 'train on line', which meant train departing Kendal. The gates had to be opened immediately, your eyes would be strained to see a light from the fire box as it came under the bridge further down the line, your ears trying to detect the sound of the engine, then when it eventually came 'towards the cabin it came slowly just like a ghost train, I used to muse to myself - really spooky!! I must hasten to add that all this was forgotten when spring and summer came, working in such a lovely area within the Lake District made it all worthwhile.

Another duty I performed, was called 'lamping the signals' which protected our crossing. This was done once a week, when the lamps had to be taken out of the signals, filled with paraffin, the wicks trimmed, red and green glasses cleaned and the lamps put back. This task involved climbing up and down the signal ladder, quite a nerve racking job especially in windy weather, as some of the signals were over sixty feet in height, with no back rest. This job had to be done, because if you missed doing it, the signal lights would not show in darkness and you would, quite rightly, be reported by the train drivers for not doing your duty.

I had a signal at the crossing which was called the 'distance signal' and was situated about half a mile from the crossing, which meant quite a long walk but when the day came for me to 'lamp' this particular signal, I used to pick the time of day when it was a quiet period, meaning no trains due. I would get my cycle out and when it was nice my son, Stephen, would accompany me on the seat on the crossbar and our collie, 'Bryn', would run beside us, as we cycled down the side of the railway line or the 'cess' as we called it, carrying a fresh lamp in one hand.

The telephone we had in the cabin at the crossing was on a through line from Oxenholme to Windermere, so if you wished to ring Kendal signal box for some reason, you would lift the receiver and quite often you would find somebody else already using the line, so you had to wait until they had finished, then dial the code for the signal box and make your call. There used to be some quite interesting conversations or discussions going on and of course, the problem was, you just never knew who could be listening in!!

Burneside Station taken on 18 August 1962. The small waiting room is the building on the left of the picture and the signal box is on the right.

Preston Whiteley Collection

Relaying the line at Staveley Level Crossing - note the old crane and large workforce of railwaymen with their coats hanging up on the left.   Preston Whiteley Collection

My other resident crossing keeper colleague at Staveley Level Crossing, was Charlie Malin. Charlie had worked at Birmingham New Street Station prior to coming to Staveley. His accent used to fascinate me. As I came from Carlisle, I was used to Carlisle, Scottish and Geordie accents, so this was completely different. I met Charlie and his wife Chris only twice, in all the time we lived at Burneside, yet we must have spoken a hundred times and more on the internal phone. I once asked him why he had come to this part of the country and he said he had just wanted a completely different way of life. Alas, Charlie is no longer with us.

Cyril Blair, was the other crossing keeper at Staveley, living in the village. We became acquainted more with Cyril after he left his crossing keeper's job and joined the Permanent Way Department, as a platelayer. He used to come and see us when he was working near Burneside and became a great favourite with my small son, Stephen, who had been very ill with whooping cough. Cyril was adept at whittling wood and making penny whistles from wood. Stephen would sit wide-eyed watching him as the whistle took shape. Cyril tested it and gave it to Stephen, who needless to say used to 'pipe' on it for hours. In those days, the early sixties, Staveley was a very busy crossing. The main road to Windermere and the Lakes went over it and it was quite a familiar sight to see forty to fifty vehicles standing each side of the crossing in the height of the summer, when the gates were closed for a train to pass. Today it is reasonably quiet, the crossing is now automated and a by-pass has been built, avoiding Staveley village altogether.

Our level crossing at Burneside, was on the 'high load diversion route' along which the Police used to divert high loads that could not go under the low railway bridge at Kendal Station. These vehicles were diverted off the main A6 road at Skelsmergh, just north of Kendal and routed down through the village of Burneside, over our crossing and up onto the A591 Windermere road and back into Kendal and vice versa.

We had some quite harrowing experiences with some of these loads as we were never notified beforehand that this was going to be taking place. The first we knew sometimes, was if we were lucky enough to be looking out and saw a police motorcyclist, with his lights on going slowly over the crossing a few minutes before the large load would appear. Our main worry was always safety. Was a train due and how long a load of this size would take getting over the crossing? If we were ever in any doubt whatsoever, we played safe and made it wait until the train had passed. This did not make us too popular with other motorists who were stuck behind the load but it was better to be safe than sorry. We never had any real damage to speak of, apart from the gateposts being knocked slightly out of line. The railway authorities were not too pleased if we had to delay a train by letting one of these loads over, without first letting the signalman know each side of the crossing, namely Windermere and Kendal, which is only right owing to safety.

This road diversion also proved a useful shortcut for Glasgow holiday traffic coming back from their holidays in the Lake District on Saturdays during July. Phyllis was often asked for hot water, for filling baby's bottles, flasks and even toilet facilities in emergencies, whilst they were held up waiting at the gates for a train to go through.

Of course working the crossing, we used to have our favourite drivers, especially concerning the last train into Windermere. The coaches were always left at Windermere and the engine came back 'light' to the then engine shed, at Oxenholme and of course, the sooner it left, the sooner we were able to close up and go to bed, so obviously we liked the drivers who didn't waste any time in doing so.

The best driver, from our point of view of finishing, was Ted Fothergill. He never bothered to go on the turntable, take water or anything. Ted came back so fast, it was always advisable to open our gates when he left Windermere because it was quite safe to say, it would just take him approximately ten minutes from leaving, to passing through our crossing. It was common knowledge, that when the engine went in the shed, it never required the firebox to be cleaned out as it had all blown out of the funnel on the way from Windermere!

Then there was another driver, who was just the opposite. He always insisted on going on the turntable, taking water and then he and his fireman would probably have a 'brew' and when he eventually did leave, he would probably travel about 10 mph in all, taking about thirty minutes to pass the crossing. Occasionally, this driver could be faster than our favourite driver, especially on the nights when he was going to a 'Pie and Pea Supper' after he finished, then it was a different story, he could not get on his way quickly enough, turntable, water etc were all forgotten, which was fine for us. We certainly got finished earlier. We always wished he had an appointment like that every time he was on the last train!

Once though, taking short cuts in procedure, didn't prove successful for one particular train driver and his fireman. This concerned an excursion train one Sunday which had disposed of its train at Windermere and the engine was coming back 'light' to Carnforth and they should have entered the turntable to turn and taken water for the tender. However, the driver and fireman were in such a hurry to get finished, they did not bother to do either. They shouted to the signalman to get them a 'clear' road to Carnforth and they set off at high speed going 'tender first', hoping the water they had in the tender would last until they got to Carnforth. So when it was well on its way, the signalman rang me to tell me to open my gates in good time, as they were in a hurry, so I did what he said.

Well, being in the height of summer, quite a number of cars had started to queue up at the crossing and when about twenty minutes after leaving Windermere, there was no sign of the engine, I decided to ring the signalman at Windermere and told him it had not passed me yet. He was just as puzzled as I was, as to where it had got to. So I put my signals to danger and opened the crossing gates to let all the traffic over, as quite a few of the car drivers were understandably getting quite irate. After the noise of the traffic had died down, I heard what I could only describe as a hissing sound which to me could only mean an engine at a stand somewhere. I quickly realised that it was standing in Burneside Station, which was at least five hundred yards from the crossing. I set off up the line to see what the trouble was, only to find the driver running back and forwards from a store room on the station, carrying a fire bucket in each hand, full of water and passing them up to the fireman, who was on the tender pouring the water in. In normal circumstances, a steam locomotive requires approximately 3,500 gallons, so they were obviously going to be there quite a while, to put it mildly! After about another half an hour, they decided to take a chance to see if they could make it to Carnforth. I did not hear any more from them, so they obviously made it. How they explained it on arrival at Carnforth I never knew but I shall never forget the look on their faces, of sheer panic and frustration, sweating profusely and wondering at the same time if they would make it back or not! Mission impossible accomplished!

I remember the incident at Windermere Railway Station when a passenger coach crashed through the buffers and station wall, into the forecourt at 12.30 pm on Monday 13 August 1962, as I was working at the crossing at the time. John Jackson was the signalman on duty that day at Windermere, a nice chap who took everything in his stride. I was speaking to John on the phone, just as it happened, all he said was, "I'll have to leave you, I think the 'Blackpool' has run through the wall on to the street outside!" I put the phone down trying to figure out what exactly had happened.

The train in question, was the 'summer only' through train from Blackpool to Windermere, a steam train comprising of eight coaches. The normal procedure at Windermere, was that the engine would pull the empty coaches out of the station to the top of the slight gradient to the signal box, where it was detached and the 'strings' were then pulled on all the coaches, to release the vacuum out of them. Then gravity took them back down into the station platform, then they were braked by the hand brakes in both brake vans, the front and rear coaches.

For some reason these brakes were not applying themselves sufficiently enough to hold, with the result that both shunters who were in the brake vans realising this, managed to jump out clear and let them go, hence the crash.

Miraculously no one was killed or injured, had the weather been wet, the crash would probably have resulted in injury at least, to people who normally shelter under the awning outside, waiting for buses. There was concern for a young man who was seen repairing his bicycle before the crash but he was discovered fit and well.

This caused utter chaos to the services to and from Windermere throughout the rest of that day and a good few days after. That particular night because of the amount of breakdown trains etc running to and from, we didn't finish until 2 am in the morning. I went through to Windermere a few days later to see for myself what damage had been caused. It really was quite horrendous and after the damage was eventually cleared, all that was left was a large gaping hole in the wall, which was repaired a few months later just prior to a visit from Princess Margaret.

My father had retired as a guard at Carlisle Station on his 65th birthday. He had loved his job. He died, sadly, in 1963 aged 68 years. My mother eventually moved to a bungalow in Morton Estate, Carlisle, where she lived until she died in 1983, aged 86 years.

Quite a lot of people used to ask me over the years, "Oxenholme Station 1965, did I remember the shooting there?" Yes, I remember it well, a very tragic affair. I was still living and working at Burneside Level Crossing and it concerned the shooting of three policemen, at 3 am on Wednesday 10 February 1965, outside the waiting room on platform No 1, at Oxenholme Station. One police officer was killed and the other two police officers were wounded by a gunman, who had apparently committed a robbery in Kendal the night before.

The only railwayman on duty at Oxenholme during that night, was the signalman, Jack Swainbank who was in No 2 signalbox, which was situated just off the south side of platform No 1. Jack had apparently witnessed everything that had taken place.

I remember him telling me after it was all over, that shortly after he had come on duty at 10 pm the night before, the police had come to see him and said they were searching for a man. They had returned again about 3 am and said they were going to make a further search. They went up the platform and then he heard five shots in quick succession. Next thing he saw was a policeman lying on the platform. He managed to put a light on the platform (they were still gas

An earlier picture of Windermere Railway Station
Courtesy of the Margaret Duff Collection

The accident at Windermere Railway Station on Monday 13 August 1962
Preston Whiteley Collection

No 2 signal box at Oxenhome Railway Station shown on left of picture, with a R A Riddels Standard goods train, northbound on the down line. This is the signal box where Jack was on duty during the night of the shooting, on 10 February 1965. Photo taken in 1965.   John Bateson

lamps in those days) and this enabled him to see just exactly what had happened. Jack couldn't bring himself to say anything further.

It became headline news in all local and national newspapers, two hundred policemen from four counties were engaged in a combined operation. The man was eventually caught in the vicinity of Oxenholme Station, at noon, on Wednesday 10 February 1965.

I shall always remember when I rang Jack Swainbank, at No 2 signal box at 5 am on that morning, of 10 February, to inform him that the crossing was open, which was normal practice. He just passed the time of day, as he always did, and I asked him if he had had a good night. To which he replied, "A bit hectic, I'm really tired and ready for my bed!" It was not until later that I learned what had happened. You must remember that while the incident was taking place, Jack would have trains passing his box every quarter an hour at least, this box was as busy through the night as it was during the day. The trains were expresses and quite a number of freight trains, so as I said, it must have been a traumatic and terrible night for Jack and throughout it all he had kept his cool!

I myself became involved in the situation just after informing Jack Swainbank that I was open. A young policeman came to my cabin with instructions from his bosses, that he had to sit with me until further notice and told me briefly what had happened and that the person they were after had escaped from Oxenholme and was seen running towards the Windermere line. The policeman was armed with two revolvers and told me he had been out all night. On hearing this, Phyllis, quickly provided him with a much appreciated steaming hot mug of tea and warm buttered toast. By dinnertime it was all over. Quite a morning for us all but I will always remember Jack, as that modest and very brave signalman, who kept his nerve even under all the stress of the situation.

Our neighbours at this time, were Mr & Mrs John Scott, of Hollins Farm, Burneside, who had a dairy herd. They had six sons and a daughter. One of the sons, Alan, worked in the dairy and Mr Scott delivered milk daily round the area. Denise our older daughter and her friend, Margaret Dawes, used to help to deliver the milk around Burneside at weekends and holidays. Nancy, our younger daughter, went to Mr & Mrs Gibson's farm with her friend, Hilary Dixon, but mainly I think to ride the farm pony 'Flash'. Burneside at this time boasted an illustrious cricket team, winning the League and were top of the Championship Table.

Whilst still at Burneside, I remember the times when the engines of Class 7 type, like the 'Evening Star', called at Kendal. On dark, wet and windy nights, you could hear the sound of the train setting off from the station towards Burneside, which was some three miles away. You would hear the driving wheels, shuddering to get to grips with the wet conditions, then that great sound of everything coordinating and 'setting off'. When the train came under the bridge nearing the railway crossing, the glow from the footplate lit up the engine and you could see the smoke and sparks belching out of the funnel and when it came over the crossing, the driver would acknowledge us. What a great sight, the sound and power emanating from that engine, made you feel really proud to be a railwayman!

Chapter Six
STATION FOREMAN AT KENDAL STATION
(1965-71)

I applied for the position of one of the station foreman jobs at Kendal in 1965, after seeing it advertised in the list of vacancies that came out every month. I got the job, we still continued living at Burneside Crossing for three years and Phyllis continued operating the level crossing together with a relief crossing man. When I first went to Burneside in 1961, I had put my name down for a council house and had gone on the waiting list. Then in 1968, South Lakeland District Council informed us that our name had come up for a house. We had a choice, either Arnside or Crosthwaite. We chose Arnside and have never regretted it. We left Burneside Crossing on 24 October 1968, on Stephen's 9th birthday, to our new home.

There had been a lot of talk of automation and a lot of changes were going on in the railways at this time, so after we left our crossing keepers' home, the house was left empty for a short while and then the railway put the cottage up for sale.

When I started at Kendal, we only had two platforms, an up and down and a bay platform, for stabling coaches in. We had a parcel office, station master's office, waiting room and the sub-way led down to the front of the station, where the ticket office was situated. We had a station master, two foremen, four parcel clerks and two shunters.

These are some of the people I worked with between 1965/71 during my days at Kendal: Les Barwise, Joe Longcake (both foremen), Frank Procter (shunter in goods yard), Syd Rumney (wagon driver), Ken Huggonson (parcel porter), George Lowthian (parcel porter), Miss Dorothy Burdett, Miss Joan Postlethwaite, Mr Joe Peruzza, Jimmy Saul (all clerks) and Mr Walter Auty (station master).

Kendal was a busy station in the late sixties/early seventies. Our main outgoing parcel traffic was mainly 'K' Shoe traffic plus Post Office parcel mail, which we loaded into eighteen parcel train vans. It used to leave every weekday night at 6.35 pm, destination London Kilburn. We also had two parcel trains a day coming in, all with parcels for delivery to Kendal and surrounding districts. That time there were six delivery rounds in the town alone, plus up to twelve or more delivery rounds to the surrounding districts, covering mostly the whole of the South Lakes area, Sedbergh and Kirkby Lonsdale.

An example of a typical day at Kendal Railway Station, would be starting at 5 am

The front of Kendal Railway Station in the 1980's.
This was closed in 1971 and stood empty for some time before development.　　*John Bateson*

Kendal Railway Station, taken on 16 April 1961. I remember them dismantling the Oxenholme
platform on the right. Two chaps and a young lass using a mechanical digger and they sold all
the lead from the roof to Hanratty's, the nearby scrap yard.
Preston Whiteley Collection

and the first train arriving at 5.30 am was the morning mail from London, stopping at Kendal on its way to Windermere. This train brought all the Post Office letter mail bags which the GPO staff collected and the morning newspapers, which were collected by John Menzies, who subsequently delivered them to the local newsagents.

The next train at 5.45 am was the parcel train which consisted of two large vans fully loaded with parcels and one fully loaded with Post Office parcel mail. The parcels were for delivery to Kendal and surrounding districts and the whole of the South Lakes. The parcel mail bags was again collected by the GPO staff and taken to their sorting office in town. After we had unloaded all the Kendal traffic, as it was called, the train then proceeded on its way to Windermere, with just the GPO parcel mail left in, even Windermere parcels were unloaded at Kendal and then delivered by road.

Our next duty was to carry each individual parcel off the platform into the parcel office and sort them into the different delivery rounds ie for Kendal. We had what we referred to as east and west rounds, meaning east and west of the River Kent (which more or less runs through the centre of Kendal). Then we had Highgate, Stramongate, Stricklandgate, these were called town rounds, then we had Windermere / Bowness, Ambleside / Grasmere, Staveley, Tebay / Grayrigg / Kirkby Stephen, Sedbergh, Kirkby Lonsdale, all large rounds and could be very difficult ones, especially in the winter months. The van drivers used to tell us of some of their experiences when they came back in at night. We would sort about 1,000 parcels every morning, with only three staff. The vans that delivered these parcels were our own British Rail Express vans from our goods yard, they were wine and yellow coloured.

Then after the last of the delivery vans had gone, the parcel office would be filled with perhaps fifteen large, four wheeled barrows, 'long backs' as we called them, ready for the hundreds of cartons of 'K' Shoes to arrive from the two factories in Kendal. Come lunch time at 12.24 pm another parcel train would arrive and we would have a repeat performance of the early morning. We also had van loads of GPO parcel mail arriving to go on the parcel train as well and I believe the Post Office had their own parcel sorting office in one of the 'K' Shoe factories.

In addition to all the duties we had to do, I, as a station foreman, had to start preparing to make the outgoing parcel train ready which was down in the sidings. This consisted of a train with eighteen large parcel vans, all to be labelled to different destinations eg Liverpool, Manchester, Carlisle, Glasgow, Peterborough, Reading, Redhill, London Kilburn etc. When after it was ready, I would bring it into the Station with the shunt engine (which was really the Kendal goods engine, usually a Black Five) and start loading up with the 'K'

An English Electric Type 4, No D326 - the 11 am Windermere Euston - known at the 'Lakes Express'. Note the number 1A - meaning Class 1; A - going to London and 34 is the number of the train. Taken in April 1961.   Courtesy of the Margaret Duff Collection

Shoes and GPO parcel mail which had arrived. Periodically, the train had to be moved to the opposite platform, every time the passenger trains arrived from Oxenholme to Windermere but after 3 o'clock in an afternoon, things really started to 'hot up'. We could have about three vans all queuing up outside the parcel office, loaded with shoes waiting to be checked in off the delivery sheets, as they came through the parcel office window. In addition to 'K' Shoes traffic, we had parcels from the other local firms in Kendal and surrounding areas ie Isaac Braithwaite (or IB's as everyone called them), Goodacre Carpets from Kendal and Holme, Gawith Hoggarth (snuff factory), Lunesdale Nurseries and many others.

The parcel train had to leave Kendal on time at 6.35 pm every weekday, destined for London Kilburn and to enable this to be achieved, the staff who were on the early shift, finished at 1 pm as normal and were asked to come back on again at 3 pm and work until 6.30 pm. These were split shifts which we worked every other week and as I was living at Arnside at the time, it was not really feasible for me to travel home and back, so it made it a long day from 4.30 am until 7 pm, when I finally got home.

The engine that used to work these parcel trains came from Preston and on two occasions we had the very same diesel locomotive, which was on the postal train

Kendal Goods Yard in the 1960's. Note Class 4F 0-6-0 loco on parcel vans in sidings on up side of Windermere line. The station itself is in the background looking towards Oxenholme. On the far left is the shunting cabin which Frank Procter used and the Class 4F was the shunt engine.

Courtesy of the Margaret Duff Collection

which was involved in the 'Great Train Robbery'. For some unknown reason, on both occasions this engine was on the train our parcel train broke down due to mechanical trouble on this locomotive. Everyone was convinced it was jinxed! In the end it was taken out of service completely.

In those days as I said, the railway used to deliver thousands of mail order catalogues and Kendal was no exception. I do believe every home in Kendal had one, as well as every farm house and village for miles around. I remember one farm that the driver had to deliver to, which involved opening and closing five gates on a two mile track, then when he eventually got to the farm, he found his vehicle was too large and there was not enough space for him to turn and he had to reverse all the way back down.

When I was working at Kendal, we had an old chap we used to work with called, Frank Proctor. He never had a car or cycle to get him to work, he used to rely on getting a lift in by lorry. He lived about six miles away at Levens and this was during the days before the motorway was built, so all the heavy overnight transport used to more or less pass by his house. Every morning he would arrive at work at about 5 o'clock but he did not officially start until 7 o'clock. He was well known and highly thought of by these drivers. When we held his retirement party, one of the gifts Frank received, was an envelope containing money which the lorry drivers had all donated. Frank was quite overwhelmed by it all. He was quite a character!

I lived in Arnside but never had the pleasure of working at the railway station there, though it was a bustling thriving place, with two porters and a booking clerk, and even used to have its own station master. At one time all trains stopped there. The Royal train, 'The Grove' was stabled there one night in 1970, when the Queen and Duke of Edinburgh were on their way to Barrow-in-Furness, to launch a nuclear submarine. This was kept very low key but security was, of course, high. The following morning at 4.15 am the Police stopped and checked me as I was going to work. That evening I discovered why. Stephen, my son, told me that his primary school had turned out to wave goodbye to the Queen and Duke of Edinburgh who left by train enroute to Barrow for the nuclear submarine launch.

Kendal Station, like many at that time, was sadly run down and eventually closed in 1971 and is now an unstaffed halt. The station buildings have been refurbished and used as a chemist and doctor's surgery (Station House Surgery). The goods warehouse is now an Age Concern Shop and Fitted Kitchen premises, the sidings and railway lines have all gone and is now an industrial estate. The staff were all made redundant but most applied for and got other jobs within the area.

Chapter Seven
GUARD AT MORECAMBE
(1971-76)

I applied for and got, the job of guard, at Morecambe when I saw it advertised. It was within easy travelling distance from home. When I went to Morecambe Promenade Station in 1971, this was a very busy station indeed, with thirty drivers and fifteen guards. The station staff included: two station inspectors, two shunters, two booking clerks and six porters. The station was large, it had four platforms, big refreshment room, large booking office and two big waiting rooms, ladies and gents toilets and a ladies waiting room attendant.

Morecambe had three Belfast Boat Trains running into it, to and from Heysham Harbour Station, morning and night, every day of the week, except Sundays, connecting with the boat to Belfast. The 'Ulster Express' as it was called, went to London, another to Manchester and the last one to Leeds and vice-versa for the night sailing. I was mostly involved with the Leeds one. We used to leave Leeds at 9.10 pm arriving at the harbour at 11 pm. It always comprised of an eight coach DMU and was always a full train. In addition, there was a half hourly service to and from Lancaster, all through the day and a good service to and from Leeds. Excursion trains also came from Glasgow and all over at weekends.

When our train arrived in Leeds, we used to have to go by bus from Leeds City Station to Neville Hill Carriage Sheds, to work our empty coaches back to Leeds City Station, which were to form our train back to Morecambe. Fortunately though, through no fault of our own, we got out of doing that part of the job when the bus people found out what we were carrying in our guard's bag. Along with other things, were twelve detonators as part of our equipment, for protecting our train and they banned us from using the bus and informed British Rail accordingly. So we never saw Neville Hill ever again. I think the bus people let their imaginations run riot and imagined a bus being blown up or something, which would not of course have happened.

On Saturdays, in the summer season, we got a great influx of holiday makers all bound for 'Pontins' Holiday Camp, at 'Middleton Towers'. It was nothing out of the ordinary to see four or five double decker buses, lined up outside the station waiting to transport them all to the camp.

There was one chap, who used to work on the station, called Jack Stainton and what a character he was. I used to call him 'Mr Morecambe', he seemed to do everything ie ticket collecting, bill posting, left luggage attendant, carriage

An old photo of a 3 car set at Heysham Station in its heyday.
Taken on 17 August 1963   Preston Whiteley Collection

The same train LNWR electrics No M 28221 M between Lancaster Green Ayre and Scale Hall
taken two years later in August 1965   Preston Whiteley Collection

cleaning, you name it, Jack did it. His bark was worse than his bite, as passengers used to find out. I remember one particular very busy Saturday morning at about 9.30 am and I was working the 10 am to Leeds. This was always a very busy train with people going home after their holidays. Jack was in full swing as you can imagine, he had them all lined up in the concourse, one queue for Leeds and Bradford, another queue for Lancaster and stations south. The first train to run in was for Lancaster and Jack yelled at the top of his voice, "Lancaster Train!" At which all the passengers in the queue immediately picked up their cases and started to proceed through the barrier which Jack had opened for them, only to be stopped by the Leeds and Bradford passengers, who wanted to get through as well. Seeing this great surge of passengers, Jack shouted again very loudly, "I said Lancaster train! Are you Yorkshire folk all hard of hearing? It never ceases to amaze me, that you are always last to arrive for your week's holiday, you want to be the first to leave and you intend to spend as little as possible in between!" They were all more or less senior citizens and took it in good humour and probably had heard it many times before over the years. I doubt whether this Sgt Bilko attitude would be accepted today and sadly Jack is another of that generation of railwayman, who is no longer with us.

Phyllis and I went to his funeral and couldn't help but smile, when the vicar mentioned in his sermon about Jack being such a character who would always be remembered for his good natured banter with the passengers. No doubt, Dame Thora Hird would remember him, as she often used to travel from her home in Morecambe on the 'Ulster Express' to London.

When the 'Menai Bridge' was badly burned trains running to Holyhead for Dun-Laoghaire, had to be diverted to Heysham and made it very busy at that time. I know that before they stopped the sailings to Belfast, Heysham was getting very tight on security re the IRA situation. The police and army were always 'on their toes' keeping an eye on everything and everybody that moved, even us, so it was a great relief at times to leave the station behind.

I remember one particular morning, I was working the Leeds boat train out of Heysham and on board was a young woman who was very heavily pregnant and had a little girl about five years old with her. She was enroute to Sheffield, having just arrived off the boat from Belfast and was as she put it "Getting away from the IRA bombing."

Well, we were well on our way when the van door opened and a young girl came to inform me that there was a lady towards the front of the train about to have a baby, so I quickly made my way to see her and on my way asked if there happened to be a nurse or doctor on board. Luckily, a lady doctor came to my assistance, took one look at the mother-to-be and informed me, we would have to get her to the nearest hospital as soon as possible. So I told the driver to stop at the next signal box, to wire the station ahead to have an ambulance standing by and happily she had her baby half an hour after arriving at hospital. She had a bouncing, little baby boy and called it John after the driver and myself, who shared the name, John. Lovely, but quite nerve racking all the same.

Railwaymen generally had a good sense of humour but sadly not everybody took it the way it was intended. This happened, when a Leeds driver got into the driver's cab of a full Diesel Motor Unit of passengers, carrying a white stick and wearing dark glasses. When he looked round the train had emptied and all his passengers were standing on the platform. Sadly, he got three day's suspension for that incident!

Morecambe Promenade Station sadly closed in 1976, probably partly caused by Heysham closing and the end of the Belfast sailings, which had formed a great deal of our business. Once again people were made redundant, again being offered the option of applying for other jobs within British Rail and some near retirement just took it.

Chapter Eight
OXENHOLME TO RETIREMENT
(1976-95)

I was fortunate to get a job at Oxenholme in July 1976, when I was made redundant at Morecambe, as I had heard that three men were retiring that year and put in for one of the posts. I was lucky and started as a 'general purpose relief'.

At the station, we had a main up and down platform, as well as a side platform for Windermere departures. There was a booking office, foreman's office, large modern waiting room, staff room, toilets on the up platform and small waiting room on the down platform and later in the 1980's we also got a buffet.

My duties involved working at Oxenholme, Windermere and a small crossing at Lambrigg, which is situated on the West Coast Main Line, between Oxenholme and Grayrigg. I used to cover at the crossing, during holidays and sickness.

This job at Lambrigg was a very lonely one. The crossing was manned 24 hrs a day, seven days a week. The hours were earlies, lates and nights and to allow one man to have a weekend off, you worked from 10 pm on a Saturday until 8 am on a Sunday. Then back again on Sunday at 7 pm until 6 am Monday, then again at 2pm until 10 pm and the other man did 8 am until 7 pm on Sunday.

The job consisted of just sitting in a small cabin and if you were lucky, you could maybe have two calls in eight hours, requiring to go over the actual crossing. When this happened, you had to ring the power box at Carlisle and they gave you permission to open the gates, making sure you told them immediately the vehicle had gone over and you had closed the gates again to the road. On the night shift especially, you maybe never even had one vehicle over the crossing in the whole time. In the summer the regular men each had an allotment, which kept them busy. They also erected a small garage for their cars. I'm sure, they had the cleanest, shiniest cars in the area!

I remember one Sunday, I was on duty from 8 am to 7 pm and it was the middle of January. It was a lovely morning but by about 2 pm it had begun to cloud over, it started to snow heavily and by about 5 pm it was about three to four feet deep and I was beginning to get a little concerned as to how I was going to get home. My mate Jimmy Brunskill arrived to take over. He had set off from Low Gill Station where he lived, about five miles away and told me that he had been skating all over the road to get here and had left the car at the bottom of the lane, at Docker Brow. He advised me to leave my car where it was. I rang the power

Lambrigg signal box/crossing where I spent many hours. This had only point levers in it.
Preston Whiteley Collection

Windermere Railway Station on a busy day, 4 June 1963 - No's 45699 Class 5XP;
42571 Class 4T and D303 Class 40 Diesel.   Preston Whiteley Collection

*Platelayers busy at Oxenholme Station on 3 June 1962 with a Class 6, 4-6-0,
No 46101 on No 2 platform, northbound.   Preston Whiteley Collection*

*The Royal Scot, 'City of Glasgow', passing through Oxenholme.
The former lamp room is seen on the left taken in 1960's.   Alec Mayor*

box at Carlisle and explained my predicament to them. They could not believe that we had so much snow, as there was nothing at Carlisle, a lovely moonlight night as they put it! Nevertheless, they kindly arranged for a train to stop especially for me and drop me off at Carnforth, where I got the train home to Arnside, arriving home at 11 pm. What a day! Eventually the County Council redirected the road and Lambrigg was closed and today the old crossing gates form part of the fence.

I was working relief at Windermere, on a very busy Saturday in mid-July 1976, we had approximately two hundred and fifty to three hundred people standing on the platform, mostly tourists of every nationality. The train arrived and everyone just about managed to board the two coach Diesel Motor Unit. After a while we heard both engines suddenly stop. The driver tried again and again to get them to start but all to no avail and he declared the train a complete failure. I then had the task of conveying the bad news to the passengers and asking them if they would all very kindly leave the train and we would try and arrange alternative transport ie by road.

We have at Windermere a local coach company, called 'The Mountain Goat' and their office was situated next to the station. Bearing this in mind, the booking clerk had heard about our trouble and had come onto the platform and shouted, "I'll get them a couple of mountain goats!" He immediately left running back into the office to phone. While he was doing this, there was a knocking at the window and it was an American gentleman, with a very puzzled expression on his face, inquiring whether he had heard us correctly, "Did you say the train had broken down and you were getting us a mountain goat?" He went onto say, that he and his wife were kinda on the hefty side, they had travelled on all kinds and modes of transport in their travels ie camels and elephants, but never on a goat and what about all the luggage they had with them? It then became clear to us, we had not realised in our panic or haste, call it what you may, that we had not made it clear at the time, that the mountain goat was a coach company and it was a coach we were getting them. I shall never forget the relief on the couples faces, it was really a pleasure to see and all the rest of the passengers because they were mostly foreigners. I think they all imagined a couple of goats coming down from the fells for them. The coach staff tell me that even today the Americans in particular, always make sure when they have booked their tour with them, that it's a coach they have booked and not the four legged variety! Word must have got around fast in America, that we do some peculiar things in this country, as far as travel is concerned!

I became senior railman in November 1977 and this job was later renamed to chargeman. Here is an example of a typical day at Oxenholme that I could be faced with, when everything that can go wrong does go wrong! The early shift began at 5.45 am and the staff comprised of myself, one porter and a booking clerk. The first problem that confronted us, was that the first train to Windermere had broken down at Carnforth and we were not likely to get a replacement for at least two hours. Well, the railways never really had any contingency plans that we could fall back on, we just had to use our common sense and resolve it the best way we could and, of course, as quickly as possible. We started ringing the local taxi firms and asking them if they could assist us as our train had broken down. Luckily for us, we did have some great blokes who would turn out at any time to help us. So it was just a case of sending taxis to the three stations between Oxenholme and Windermere, as they were all unstaffed and there was no way of informing, the passengers that the train had broken down. They would all be expecting to connect with the London train, which was running on time, so it was a question of whether the taxis would make it back in time to connect with this train. We were not allowed to hold up a connecting train over a certain time, British Rail took the overall view, that it was not feasible to hold up a train carrying maybe five hundred passengers, for the sake of a couple of taxis with probably six passengers, regardless of the circumstances involved. Unfortunately, at the end of it all, myself, porter and booking clerk, were all held personally to blame!

We managed at last to get a train on the Windermere branch line, so all was now back to normal for at least two hours or so, until an Intercity train arrived at Oxenholme and the engine broke down. Well, not exactly broke down but for some reason the driver was unable to get it into forward gear, so after about half an hour of using different methods still to no avail, it was decided to detrain all the passengers and reverse the whole train into the sidings. This was done, firstly to clear the line and secondly to enable other trains standing behind to pass, which I should imagine, there must have been at least half a dozen by now. This is you will remember the West Coast Main Line, a very busy line at anytime of day or night.

The position we found ourselves in now, was one of utter chaos to say the least! We had two hundred and fifty to three hundred people on the platform, all with different destinations to go to, with just myself and a porter on the platform and the clerk in the office, to answer all their questions (and there were plenty), as you can imagine! Imagine two hundred and fifty people all around you, inquiring what I was going to do with them, which I had to admit I had no idea, until I was allowed to get back to my office and find out what trains we had following, where they were going, where they were calling at on leaving Oxenholme and, of course, the main question I would be asked, "What time would they arrive?" This is the kind of situation where railway staff are frequently accused of not giving information and where there is nobody on hand to give it immediately. Bearing in mind, there was only one member of staff on duty on that particular platform, the only other member of platform staff was on the other platform, where trains were all running normally into the station and had to be attended to. Quite a stressful time, when you are put under a lot of severe pressure, in more ways than one!

Here are a few examples of the problems we were faced with in cases like that: ascertain people's train connections and whether they would be maintained. I never guaranteed this, as I always found that this was the biggest bone of contention amongst passengers whatever the situation. I allowed passengers to use our telephone, mainly to reassure the people who were going to be meeting them, that they were alright but would be delayed.

We always aimed to do our best to inform our passengers when the next train was due to arrive, where it was bound for and of course all the stations ahead of us were now fully aware of what had occurred at Oxenholme and would be making their own arrangements, as this failure would have a fairly long term effect on services throughout the rest of the day. Usually, after two or three hours everyone was on their way again and things were reverting slowly back to normal.

Finally, came the problem of disposing of the disabled train out of the siding, as the set of coaches particularly, all worked on a circuit working. This means that if this set did not get its return working, it could cause problems at its planned destination (lack of coaches at that end). So it was imperative that these coaches were dispatched as soon as possible. Of course in this case it involved waiting for a replacement engine to arrive.

That was quite a day and just one example of what it could be like at Oxenholme, on a 6 am to 2.15 pm shift in particular and if you did not keep your nerve, it could really get to you, where you just felt like running away from it all!

Another night I was on duty, we had a different set of problems to deal with. My assistant had, unfortunately gone home sick and I had a train broken down on the Windermere branch line between stations. The weather was bad, it was pouring down with rain, an Intercity train from London had failed at Carnforth and a train from Glasgow was running approximately two hours late. There were about a dozen people standing in the booking office requiring tickets etc. Both internal and public telephones were ringing incessantly. I just stood for a moment, gathering my thoughts, wondering what to do first and decided to answer the public phone first. I got what sounded like a very sweet old lady, wishing to know the times of trains to Carlisle the next day, could I very kindly give her two trains, not too early and two back later in the day, say probably two or three hours, just time to do a little shopping and could I give them to her slowly as she was a little deaf and not very quick at writing.

So with all hell letting loose around me, people in the booking office glaring at me through the window. People on the platform wondering where the London train had got to that I had previously announced as running on time, Windermere train broken down enroute somewhere between Oxenholme and Windermere full of passengers and wondering at the same time, whether the train from Glasgow had lost more time. First things first! I commenced to give my sweet little lady the information she required, for which she thanked me heartily and wished me a peaceful night!! Little did she know that as soon as I put the phone down, I was going to enter utter chaos! Still with a bit of patience and luck, call it what you may, it all got sorted out by the end of the night. I know one thing, I went home completely shattered and hoped I would never ever get a repeat of that particular set of circumstances!

I remember another time when we had our problems at Oxenholme and I was working this particular night, with Bob Smith, an Australian, who worked with us for a time. He had worked for the railways back in Australia and what was about to take place must have seemed pretty strange to him, as it certainly did to me!

It concerned the 15.30 hrs train from London due to arrive Oxenholme at 18.45 hrs. We were informed that it was running on time but had not called at Lancaster. The reason being a freight had broken down in the platform where this train was to have called and rather than keep it standing outside the station until such time as they were able to remove the freight train, it was decided to run our train nonstop through the middle line of the station and bring the Lancaster passengers to Oxenholme, where they would have approximately five minutes to wait for a train back to Lancaster. We could not believe this was happening but there was nothing we could do about it.

What the control people did not bargain for, was that the south bound train had failed on its way down Shap, making it at least forty minutes late, so it was left to my Australian friend and myself to inform the Lancaster passengers on arrival, that they could easily expect an hour's wait.

Well, as far as Bob Smith and I were concerned we thought our time had come and we were going to be 'lynched'. All the passengers were in a very irate state to say the least, when they alighted at Oxenholme. They almost buried us with questions and of course there was a few 'Victor Meldrews' amongst them! Many demanded taxis at our expense, of course, to take them back to Lancaster and stated they could not believe it, when the train went whizzing through Lancaster, for they had not been informed of the reason until they were nearing

Oxenholme Station, taken from railway bridge on 17 July 1987. Note No 2 signal box has now gone. Large building on right behind the wall is a car repairers garage. On the left is the Windermere branch line and my old Ford Cortina Estate is also there!

Courtesy of the Margaret Duff Collection

Oxenholme. After this little escapade, the control people never tried anything like that again, needless to say, it was left to myself to try and explain someone else's folly!

Ever since I started at Oxenholme in 1976, the West Coast Main Line has been closed on Sundays between Preston and Carlisle for essential engineering to take place between midnight until approximately 3 o'clock on Sunday afternoons. This took place during the winter months, with the exception of Christmas, when we did get a train service. The rest of the time these trains were diverted via the Settle and Carlisle and Blackburn to Preston lines. We, at Oxenholme had the convenience of a double decker Ribble bus service in place of a train. One bus travelled to Preston via Lancaster and the other bus travelled to Carlisle via Penrith. This was considered a way of life on Sundays. I remember one Sunday, the comedian Bob Monkhouse had booked his ticket with us and when he obtained his ticket, he inquired which platform his train would leave from, only to be told by the booking clerk, Ken Bateson, "It's not a train but a bus, sir and it leaves from the station forecourt, just through the gate!" To which Bob Monkhouse smiled and was heard to say, "There's a joke in there somewhere, I'm sure!"

This arrangement did have its embarrassing moments and unfortunately not everyone accepted the arrangements quite so well. I remember one who didn't. It involved a very 'well to do' sort of gentleman, who had just booked a first class return ticket to London, which was over £100 at the time, only to be told that the first part of his journey would be by double decker bus to Preston. He was totally unaware of this situation, he became very irate and asked again when he could get a train to take him to London, only to be told there was nothing until 4.30 pm, bearing in mind it was only 12 noon at the time. He stormed back into the booking office and demanded his money back. We tried without much success to explain that this work had to be done and Sundays was the only time it could be carried out and could only apologise for this disruption. He left under his own steam!

There were other times when we had to depend on buses when a train had failed, particularly on the Windermere branch line and frequently we were required to get a bus to meet the last train from London, when it was running very late and we were unable to keep the last connection to Windermere. I can honestly say the Ribble bus people never let us down once. There were three good lads, whom I could call upon day or night and I knew would always help - Nigel Loynes, David Uttley and John Abbott, they helped us out of some difficult situations. It was not the easiest of runs to Windermere via bus, especially when they were required to call at all the stations enroute. Burneside and Staveley Stations in particular, were not the easiest of places to manoeuvre a bus into and remember they were running in place of the train in some cases, so they had to keep running according to the timetable but somehow these lads always seemed to manage it!

We also had some good taxi drivers, who used to stand at Oxenholme Station. During the early eighties, there was one firm called 'Garry's Taxis', owned then by Lennie Edgar and his partners, John and Alfie, who would turn out anytime they were needed and went on occasions for me to Preston, Edinburgh and Blackpool. Nothing was ever too much trouble to them. I once requested Lennie to meet a train with me which should have been in at 11 pm and did not arrive until 4am. We knew it had some passengers on for Barrow-in-Furness and we were obliged to get them to their destination, as it was our fault the train was late.

We also had a firm called, 'Blue Star Taxis', which set up a 24 hr office at the station, which was very convenient for us. I have known a few times when we had trains running late, especially at night and they provided us with maybe six taxis at any one time and always very good. John Phillipson had one taxi and he went under the name, 'Royal Scot Taxis' and was also good to know. The other firm that obliged, was 'Kendal Taxis', owned by Alan Barnes and many's the time they used to sit all night outside the station waiting for business, as they were totally reliant on people coming off the trains. On one occasion Alan's taxi was the only one standing on the ramp, when we had a lady who was travelling to the very north of Scotland and the last connection to get her there, left Edinbugh early afternoon and we had no train to get her there. I got authority to get her a taxi and Alan got the job of taking her there. That was the luck of the draw and they had to be prepared to go anywhere at anytime!

I have done my share of platelaying, or in laymen's terms 'working on the line' in my time and always of course on Sundays. So I have seen both sides of working and dealing with the problems of these delays. When the Permanent Way Department (the permanent way being the rails, sleepers and ballast that make up the track of a railway system), did not get enough of their own staff to perform a fairly large job on a Sunday, they used to ask if any staff from other departments were prepared to come out and help. You were paid the same rate as the platelayers, double time, so that was another attraction, because we only got paid time and three quarters on our own job. We were never asked to do any of the skilled work, we just more or less did the labouring tasks. We had some really rough ones, as well as some easy ones, a lot depended on the weather, which of course was never taken into consideration and we would work whether it was rain, hail or snow.

I remember one particularly wet and cold Sunday morning in the middle of

January, in the 1970's and I turned out with them at 5 am. There must have been approximately two hundred men altogether, it was a large relaying job or something of that nature. The inspector in charge was allocating all the different jobs out, when I heard my name being called out. He asked if I would be the 'can lad' for the day. This job involved lighting and looking after the fires, boiling the kettles and such like. I couldn't believe my luck, a cold wet morning such as it was and all I had to do was look after about six fires in a warm cabin and see that I had all the kettles boiling when the men stopped for their break, leastways that's what I thought, how very wrong I could be!

The first break went off fairly well considering. I managed to have all the kettles boiling, about ten large black ones in all, so the men went back to work all happy and that was when the trouble started. Water had to be found from somewhere. We were between Grayrigg and Shap, miles from anywhere and I realised this job of 'can lad' was not going to be as attractive as I first thought, the nearest place where I hoped I could get water was a farm situated about six large fields away from the railway line.

I found myself in the situation where I had ten large kettles to fill, four fires to tend, my biggest worry being the two hundred men to cater for and all due to break for their lunch, sandwiches etc about 12.30 pm. The time now was 10 am and all I had in my possession to carry water in, was a two gallon plastic container. So, off I set across the fields towards a farm unaware what kind of reception I would get on arrival at the farm gate. I was met by two vicious looking sheepdogs which both seemed reluctant to let me enter. The farmer appeared after hearing all the commotion, calmed the dogs down, which no doubt had been protecting their home and I explained my predicament to him and he kindly pointed me in the direction of the water tap in the farm yard. Goodness knows what he thought!

I only managed to get one kettle boiling and needless to say, I was never asked to do the 'can lad's' job ever again. I was absolutely shattered that night when I got home. I was informed later, that one of the buses there had been fully equipped with a ten gallon tank of water and was parked alongside where the cabin was situated!

I went along on other occasions with them travelling quite long distances, mostly on Saturday nights/Sunday mornings. We would leave our home station, which was at that time Kendal, about 8 pm on a Saturday night and travel by special bus to a site of work, maybe in East Lancashire or further afield, probably arriving about midnight, ready to start work and finish about 10 am or 11 am on a Sunday morning and then the long trek home, arriving about 2 pm in the afternoon. Long shifts!!

I think the worst job for me personally was what they called levelling ballast. This involved levelling the ballast that had been dropped in fairly large quantities between the rails, the 'four foot' as it was called, by shovel. This had to be levelled out down to sleeper level. Well, to do this fairly, every man was allocated eight beds each to level out and everyone had to finish his eight before they would 'lap over' as it was termed. With the result, I being the novice on the job, I was always the last to finish my eight and when I did, they all immediately 'lapped over' with the result, I was never getting a breather at all in between, only to find another eight looking at me. To make matters worse, the Inspector had a nasty habit of following up behind and accidentally tripping up, shouting the words, "Who has been in these eight? Yes, it was yours truly and he would make me go back to them, stating that they looked like graves and shouting, "I would like them level with the sleepers, if you don't mind!"

It was a real nightmare of a job and I was never able to straighten my back until Wednesday of the following week and when the weather was really hot, they would come along the line with a bucket of water and one small cup. You were only allowed one cup each and you really did feel you were on a 'chain gang'. They were a great lot of lads to work with, all the work being done by pick, shovel and crowbar, all hard manual labour and now it's all thankfully mechanized.

Of all the amusing stories from the Windermere branch line, the most amusing one I think, was about the time there were elephants on the line. Yes, just that! The train was the 5 o'clock, early morning train through to Windermere from Oxenholme, with just the driver and guard on board, a two coach Diesel Motor Unit on a summer's morning in June 1977. The guard was sitting alongside the driver in the driver's cab and they were making a steady journey. The morning was a little misty and when they came round a bend they were confronted by what appeared to be three large cows on the line. They managed to stop about one hundred yards from them, the guard got out to see if he could at least clear them off the line. After a while when he didn't return, the driver grew a little worried and set of walking along the track until he heard the guard shouting to him from down the embankment. He slid down with some difficulty, to where he found him lying at the bottom in quite a lot of pain, saying that he thought he had broken his leg. The driver immediately decided to go for help and started scrambling back up the embankment. The guard shouted, "By the way, those cows in front of us, they are not cows but elephants!" The driver stopped in mid stride, thinking not only had he injured his leg, but was in a state of shock and hallucinating besides. With all this going through his mind, he continued walking along the track to the nearest phone, only to see three elephants, standing looking at him!

I had just started my shift at Oxenholme by this time, when the phone rang. It was the driver, to inform me of the predicament he was in and could I get an ambulance for his guard, who had fallen down the embankment in his eagerness to tell him, he had found three large elephants on the line! Well, on hearing this I took the phone from my ear and looked at it in disbelief at what I had heard. Had I heard right, I said to myself, because this particular driver was known for his practical jokes but I did not think so, not at 5 o'clock in the morning, surely! I dialed '999' and then came the business of having to inform the ambulance people what had occurred and I was sure they also thought that they had a 'nutter' or 'crack-pot' on the line but in the end, they must have thought I was genuine because the ambulance was at the scene in a matter of minutes and no doubt they did get it all confirmed, by the driver, elephants and all!

The explanation for the elephants taking a morning stroll was quite simple really. As you will no doubt have figured, the circus was in Kendal and these animals had apparently somehow strayed onto the railway line somewhere between Oxenholme and Kendal and this was later explained to us by the Police and circus people, who had cleared the line so that 'normal working could be resumed' Explaining to our passengers the delay to the Windermere services, was due to 'elephants on the line', received some funny looks to say the least and I bet they were thinking, 'what will they think of next!' Both the men were from Preston and are now sadly no longer with us.

Power signal boxes, eventually replaced all the manually operated signal boxes particularly on the West Coast Main Line. The one I was concerned with, was at Carlisle, which controlled every mile of railway line between Beattock, in Scotland, to Yealand, near Carnforth, in Lancashire. The next power signal box from there south, was Preston and north, was Motherwell. I was once shown round the Carlisle signal box, I saw the three panels, one which controlled north of Carlisle Station, the middle panel, Carlisle Station itself and the third panel controlled south of Carlisle, right up to nearly Carnforth, a distance of over sixty miles. Every signal and set of points was controlled from this signal box, they even had a radar trap, where they could check the speed a train was travelling at, at one particular point on the line. I saw Oxenholme on the panel and was asked if I would like to alter a pair of points there and this was me doing it at Carlisle, with simply pressing a button. I would have loved to have seen my father's face and what he thought of it! The staff I came into contact with at the Carlisle box were: Ian Holmes, Johnny Williamson, Denis Nicholson, Keith Clementson and Les Kerr who all worked there. Unfortunately, my good friend Les is no longer with us.

The only time there was a 'chink' in the power signal boxes armour, was when they lost detection on a pair of points, meaning a fault light showed up on the panel on that particular pair of points, which meant they did not know what position the points were in, whether they were set for the main line or the siding. So we had to go down to the siding and check to see what position they were in and depending on what position they were required to be in, they had to be cranked over by hand with a cranking handle which was similar to the old starting handles used in cars and then clipped. This was a terrible job, especially when it was wet weather, because you could be there for hours until the signal fitter arrived to repair them. It was a nerve racking job at times, especially when you had done what you were required to do, you then had to wave the train full of passengers over the points which you have cranked and clipped yourself, I used to close my eyes and hoped I had got it right. Fortunately you did not have to do it very often, I think, I performed this task about four times in all my time at Oxenholme. You were only asked to do this operation within 'station limits', in my case, in the immediate vicinity of Oxenholme Station.

Delays can be caused to trains by a number of reasons, engine failure, overhead lines brought down by weather or by owls flying into them or by sheer vandalism, weather conditions ie snow, flooding, fatalities, vandalism, points' failure, essential engineering and, of course, leaves on the line.

Engine failures can occur anywhere but if you are lucky and it occurs in a very large station eg Crewe, another replacement can be found without delay. When this occurs in the wilds of the countryside this can present very serious problems indeed and an hour's delay is nothing, especially when you are waiting for a replacement engine to come maybe thirty or forty miles and then when it does arrive, it has to be coupled onto the train, an air brake test has to be performed and if it happens to be a wet and windy night these are not the easiest of tasks. All this is usually done by the senior conductor on the train, as well as keeping his passengers informed of the present position, in addition, of course, to his commercial duties, issuing tickets and checking.

Overhead power lines coming down for whatever the reason can cause a major delay, not only to one train but a number, as this involves so many safety measures to be taken into account as this is a 25,000 volt wire and could be still 'live'. I recollect one instance where the wire had wrapped itself right round the engine of a train causing up to five hours' delay to that train and the others behind.

I suppose the main one which in my experience causes more aggravation, frustration, call it what you may to passengers, is engineering taking place on the track or platelaying as we called it. This, as I have already mentioned, takes place on Sundays between the hours of midnight on Saturday and 3 pm on a Sunday afternoon, that's of course if everything goes to plan. When this fails to

The 'cement train' as it was known, used to be notorious for breaking down. This one had four engines No's 31305, 47347, 37033 and 37032. This was the 6S83, 16.05 (Coy) Clitheroe to Gunnie in Scotland on 16 June 1986. The 37033 train had failed and was set back into the down goods loop and the 31 and 47 brought from Carnforth to assist to Carlisle. Gordon Wilson (Codge) was the Carnforth driver in the picture.   Jay Hartley

Coy - denotes it was a company train.

87

Another 'cement train' with problems! This one had three engines pulling it, No's 31282, 47423, 25213. These travelled from Clitheroe, in Lancashire to Gunnie in Scotland and was already 15 hrs late with probably a different set of trains on than the ones they had originally set off with. This had set off on Friday if I remember and it was now Saturday.
Photo taken on 11 March 1987.   Jay Hartley

happen is when the delays start. This is usually overcome partly by putting single line working into operation, meaning they can pass the work which has been overrun, as they term it, by using just the one line for trains to run both ways. This operation is performed by appointing a pilotman who is responsible for taking trains through on the single line one way and bringing another train the other way. For example, if there are three trains to go one way, he would normally send the first two through and accompany the third one and the same procedure with the trains standing to come through the opposite way. Of course, if this involves a long blockage, which in some cases cannot be avoided, meaning in other words, a long distance between the crossover places and this all adds up to more delay. I said this business usually takes place on Sundays but I must say before I retired, it was quite a regular sight to be seen taking place up to maybe between 4 am and 9 am every weekday morning, hence putting delays into the early morning commuter trains. Usually extra time was allowed in their running time for this work taking place, for instance a train could be half an hour late on leaving Oxenholme but be on time when it arrives at Preston.

'Leaves on the line', is very much a standing joke with the media but when you have experienced the delays and problems this can create, it is no laughing matter. One example of this we had, occurred about 6.30 pm, the end of October in the 1990's (one wet and very windy night at Oxenholme). The next train to arrive was the 6.43 pm from London, this arrived and left dead on time. I must say at the time, I did notice that it did take a little more time than they usually do to gather speed but thought no more about it. That is, until 7.10 pm when the phone rang, it was the power box at Carlisle, to inform me that that particular train had only just passed Grayrigg travelling at a speed of approximately five miles an hour. Now in normal running time to Grayrigg, this would take about ten minutes or less, so this train on that night had taken about forty minutes due to slipping on leaves on top of an already wet rail.

The position I had was as follows, I had two freight trains that had also come through in the meantime after this train and they were both already at a stand behind it and I had another train due to arrive any minute, which I was informed by the power box I was to hold in the platform until I heard further from them.

This train remained with us for about an hour before we were told the trains in front had eventually cleared. The people on the train were by now becoming very agitated, requiring to know what the delay was and us having to explain that it was 'leaves on the line' delaying the train in front. I must say, we received some very funny looks, all very embarrassing to say the least and added to this delay, was the fact that with so many trains standing in the same vicinity for so long, this created a massive pull on the overhead lines thus lowering the voltage power, causing more delay unknown to the passengers on the train. So we take 'leaves on the line' very seriously.

Steam trains of course never had this problem. The electric loco's are all superb in many respects but once you got a shower of rain, the leaves which were already on the 'top of the rail' released a sticky resin when run over and a train with approximately ten coaches in length starting off from a dead start, on a slight gradient and at that time of year when the leaves all dropped, certainly had problems. It must have been a real nightmare for a driver because there was absolutely nothing he could do about it, only hope he could keep going.

In days past, when we had steam trains we never had this particular problem and I believe it was because they always carried sand. Not only that, but there was a ganger and maybe two platelayers, who were in charge of a length of railway. Now these men took great pride in their length, seeing to matters such as overhanging branches on trees, cutting down grass on embankments and making sure everything was right, even holding contests to see who had the best length.

'Wrong type of snow' is another comment made, which gets a lot of publicity. Well, all I can say on this subject, is that the railways created the problem themselves with the business of putting the engine at the rear of the train. This is supposed to speed up the turn around time at Euston. It was called a DVT, which means Driving Van Trailer. It was designed by British Rail for push pull working with electric loco's. The problem of the engine at the rear of the train was that whilst travelling along the snow collected and fouled up the traction engine at the rear.

When I was working at Oxenholme, my twin brother was working in the booking office at Carlisle and it raised quite a few laughs when I used to collect tickets, from the passengers leaving the platform and some would say in amazement, "I was just given this ticket by you at Carlisle about an hour ago, you sure do get around!" I had the same problem when I used to travel back to Carlisle to shop or visit by train and people used to speak to me and I hadn't a clue who they were. I sometimes heard them say, "I've have just seen him in the booking office and here he is getting off the train!" Bill, no doubt, was getting the same comments as me at Carlisle, that's what happens when you have an identical twin.

Announcing trains at stations is not the easiest of jobs and I have done a little of it in my time. It's all written down for you by British Rail, all the stops the train is going to make, where the first class is situated, the dining car and buffet car facilities, etc. The difficult part comes when a train is running late, you have to

DVT (Driving Van Trailer) Intercity northbound on the down line approaching platform 2, at Oxenholme on 28 August 1991 - the front is a Class 87 and the trailer is a Class 82.
John Bateson

45. The Advanced Passenger Train (APT) or 'Tilting Train', No's 370003 and 370006. Pictured also on the right is 6Z48 with No's 25906 and 25908, which carried rock salt from Over and Wharton, Cheshire to Inverness and had problems with seepage when it rained. This leaked onto the rails and caused all sorts of problems with the signals. The 'Z' in the number denotes the train runs when required.   Jay Hartley

Taken on 12 September 1986.

give the reason why and try and give an approximate time that the train will arrive and any more relevant information you have. It's not an easy task for some people, they just do not know what to say in some cases. I was always aware of this, as I felt we had to say something no matter how we put it, as long as we kept people informed, which I believed they appreciated.

Of course they have announcements now on trains, the guard makes announcements and a very amusing story comes to mind. Someone handed the guard a deaf aid which they had found, the guard immediately announced over his tannoy, "There has been a deaf aid handed in and it can be collected from the guard at the rear of this train. If the person sitting next to you does not appear to have heard this announcement, please give him or her a shout!"

One announcement we were not permitted to make, was when there had been a fatality on the line, suicide or whatever. This was maybe just as well in our case, as one of our lads would insist on referring to an incident such as this as a 'fertility on the line', which no doubt would have raised a few eyebrows!

I remember one announcer that we had at Lancaster a few years ago, who had the gift of being able to ad-lib and made it all sound easy. For instance, if the weather was bad he would say, "Your train for Morecambe is not in yet. So stay where you are in the warm or better still, have another cup of tea and I'll give you a shout!" He was very thoughtful and I think the passengers appreciated it. It was always a treat just to sit and listen to him, as you never knew what he was going to say next.

I have made some really good friends in my time at Oxenholme, one of them being, Alec Mayor. Alec worked for the Westmorland Gazette in the accounts section, in Kendal but his first love was always railways. What Alec did not know about the workings of a steam locomotive or in later years, electric locomotives, was not worth knowing, as one day I was to find out.

Alec used to visit the station nearly every day to collect any parcels etc which had arrived for the Gazette and he was never in a hurry to leave. He would probably hang around to see two trains come and go. Well, this particular morning, Alec was there as usual, when a train arrived and came to a stand on platform No 2, when I noticed the pantograph (meaning the collapsible/adjustable framework mounted on an electric railway locomotive, for collecting current from an overhead wire), go down on the electric loco. Well, this always spelt trouble with a capital 'T'. I went up to the driver to try and find out what the trouble was, only to be told that he had all sorts of fault lights showing on his panel and he didn't have any idea what was causing it. By this time, Alec was standing nearby and I asked him if he had any idea of how to rectify the problem. I asked the driver if it was OK if my friend had a look, though Alec was reluctant to interfere. The driver quickly replied, "If he can get me on my way, tell him to come aboard!" On hearing this, Alec climbed into his cab and immediately went to work checking all kinds of switches in the engine room, when all of a sudden the pantograph went back up on the overhead wire. Alec then said to the driver, "There you are, mate. I don't think you should have any more trouble with it. It should get you home to Glasgow!" The driver thanked him warmly and to my great relief, everything was moving again, knowing only too well the upheaval that could have been caused. I asked Alec afterwards what the trouble was? He explained in rather technical terms which I didn't fully understand but I was nonetheless very grateful and glad he had been there!

The next morning, this same train came in, with the same driver waving frantically at me, so I ran up to his engine to see what he wanted. Hoping there was no further problems, whereby he asked me in a strong Scottish accent, "Who was the wee fella who found out what was wrong with my engine yesterday? 'Cos you can tell him from me, I had no more problems with it for the rest of my journey." I then told him what Alec did, to which he quickly replied, "Well, he is wasting his time, a handy wee chap to have around!" To which I agreed with him whole heartedly.

During my days at Oxenholme I had the great pleasure of meeting Prince Charles. He had made a visit to the Lake District and he was due to leave Oxenholme at 12.30 am after a banquet held in his honour, at Sizergh Castle, on the outskirts of Kendal. I had the job of preparing his train, which involved shunting it off the main link into Windermere platform, ready for him just to step onto when he arrived and what a thrill I did get when he did arrive. After Prince Charles had been introduced to the local nobility, I was standing behind everyone, when all of a sudden I heard him asking, "Now what's this chap doing, he looks as if he has been busy?" With no further ado, he held out his hand to me and shook mine very vigorously. I was really taken unawares and it was a moment I shall always remember.

The security as you can imagine was very tight throughout. After the train had departed, I was the last person to leave the station. I locked up in the normal way, got into my car, drove out of the station car park and noticed also a police car pulling away. I had twelve miles to travel to get home and during that journey, I had three different police cars following me. I inquired what it was all about, only to be told, "Just making sure you got home alright!" Everybody else at Oxenholme that night had apparently the same treatment. I could only assume, that if I had stopped off at a phone box or something it may have appeared to them highly suspicious!

Found and lost property was another thing we had to deal with. One of the notable ones that comes to mind, happened mid morning one Saturday in summer, when a train had just departed from Oxenholme and I noticed a lady's handbag lying on one of the platform seats. There did not appear to be anyone with it, so I took it into the booking office where the clerk and myself checked through the contents. There was the usual credit cards etc and various papers with the Australian Government marked on them, £750 in sterling travellers cheques, about £600 in fifty, twenty and ten pound notes, passports, one of which was English and the other Australian.

Well, to everyone's surprise we never had one enquiry for that handbag and it remained on hand with us for approximately four months. One cold night in October about 9.30 pm a lady appeared at the booking office window and very quietly asked me, had we found a handbag which she believed she had left on the station after seeing her sister off on the train last summer. I was absolutely astounded, she described everything that was in it up to the very last detail. She told me, she had felt sure she had left it at Oxenholme and that we would take care of it for her. I found this quite incredible, as to how she had managed all this time without her handbag. I informed her that unfortunately she would be without it for one more day, as she would be required to call at the booking office during office hours to collect it from the clerk and to complete all the formalities and with this, she thanked me and disappeared into the night.

Another occasion concerning lost property, involved two Chinese girls, one of them had lost her wallet containing her passport and her money, travellers cheques etc. They were intending to stay in the Windermere area for two days and then go back to London for their flight back home to China. I had these two girls with me for approximately six hours while I tried all the stations where the train had called at and they insisted on waiting until it had arrived at Glasgow, where we asked for it be thoroughly searched, to no avail. To complicate matters even more, only one of them spoke enough English and unfortunately it was not the girl who had lost her wallet. I contacted the Chinese Embassy in London and explained the situation to them, which was not straight forward and the man I spoke to did not appear to have much sympathy re the situation and more or less said that the young lady should not have lost her wallet in the first place! He, very reluctantly, advised them to report to the Embassy as soon as they arrived in London but the fact still remained, she had no rail ticket to enable her to make that journey. I was just about to get this sorted out, when the internal phone rang and it was the ladies waiting room attendant at Carlisle. She had seen the wire I had sent and had just found the wallet concerned with everything intact, and of course it was at Carlisle of all places! These girls had never been anywhere near there. We could only assume, that the person who had stolen it whilst she was on the train, had been disturbed while they had been going through it and left. Nevertheless, it was a great relief to everyone concerned, the girls were reunited with the wallet and set off happily, if not a little tired to London. A touch of the Orient, no less!

When I went to Oxenholme in 1976, our main tourists were the Americans, in the summer particularly and what a summer it was too, hot and sunny from May to September. We used to joke with the American tourists, especially when they asked for a ticket to Birmingham, we would query, was it Alabama, or Warwickshire, or Washington, was it DC or County Durham?" So it went on, they did not understand you when you said platform No 3, you had to say 'track 3' and then they understood. I remember as well during that summer, we had nearly every American asking for a 'schedule', as they termed it to Stratford-upon-Avon and one day the booking clerk and I thought we would try a little experiment on them, by asking them what was the great attraction of going to Stratford-upon-Avon? They told us that they wanted to see where William Shakespeare was born. We said, "Robbie Burns, was born there!" They knew we were wrong of course and just joking, nevertheless, you could still see them starting to mull it over in their minds. They took it in good fun and we wished them a good journey.

DMUs were coming to the end of their life in the early 1990's and there was an amusing incident that occurred to one of them travelling on the Windermere branch line. It was a very wet morning and the driver had just brought the first run into Oxenholme from Windermere. He was complaining about water leaking in from the roof onto him and his driving desk, so much so, that he was refusing to go back to Windermere, unless he got another DMU. By coincidence, there was a replacement DMU on its way but would not arrive at Oxenholme until later. We managed however to persuade him to make the journey back to Windermere with the faulty DMU, as this part of the journey didn't really present a problem, owing to the fact that the driving cab at the other end was 'rainproof'. My mate said he had just the ideal thing to solve the problem of that return journey and told him that he would get him one of our large binbags to put over his head, make two holes in it for his eyes and as it was still dark he could keep his blinds down in his cab and his passengers would not see him. With a little more persuading, our driver agreed and set off for Windermere once again.

However, when he arrived back at Oxenholme we found that it had not gone exactly to plan. Everything had gone alright until they were just about to leave Windermere, one of the cab blinds accidentally flew up to reveal the driver sitting in full view of everyone, with this large binbag over his head and totally unaware. There were a few screams from startled passengers not believing what was before their eyes. The driver quickly removed the offending article, feeling

Early DMU, standing in siding at Oxenholme, taken in 1966
John Bateson

Later DMU No 53307 which was known as a 'rogue unit' for always breaking down. Seen trying to figure out how best to couple it up to the Diesel 47137 to be taken back to Carnforth, is left to right, Garth Shuttleworth (driver), Fred Morgan (driver) and Steve Dean (guard). Taken on 1 November 1986

Jay Hartley

Celebrating 140th Aniversary of Windermere Line, BR Pacer Twin Railbus, Class 142, No 142050, 1105 ex Windermere on 17 April 1987. Everyone was dressed in Victorian costume for the day handing out pace eggs as it was Easter.   Jay Hartley

both embarrassed and angry at the same time. The guard said he had never laughed so much in his life. At the end of the day, the driver did see the funny side to it but had to take a bit of stick over it!

I remember the day when Peter Parker, the then Chairman of British Rail, announced that all senior citizens with rail cards could go anywhere in the country for free. Well, as you can imagine, the trains were all full and standing from early morning till late at night. Tempers became flared, especially from the fare paying passengers who were unable to get a seat. The dining cars were also full with senior citizens, who were under the distinct impression that this scheme included their meals which would also be free. In some cases when told this was not so, they refused to move, thus preventing fare paying passengers from obtaining a meal, which resulted in some places, the police being called in. We did hear but never did get it confirmed that at 4 am on the morning in question there were approximately 10,000 senior citizens standing in London, Waterloo Station, just waiting to go anywhere.

Experiences I have had with passengers over the years have never ceased to amaze me and I have often jokingly said, "I could write a book!" This experience or story concerns a Liverpool lady and her young daughter at Oxenholme one summer's evening. We had a train back in the 1980's, which ran from Windermere to Lancaster, normally all trains ex Windermere terminated at Oxenholme in those days, so it was always the policy on this particular train for the guard to make sure that all passengers travelling south were made aware of this and to change at Lancaster and definitely not Oxenholme. The train came and went from Oxenholme and left standing on the platform were these two ladies. I asked them where they were going? "Liverpool!" they replied. I said, "Didn't you hear the guard's announcement on the train informing all passengers travelling south to change at Lancaster." The mother said, "Yes, we had heard but we do not live in the south, we live in Liverpool and that's in the north of England." "Yes," I agreed with them but they did live south of Oxenholme. I gave up and informed them that they now had about two hours to wait for a train south, or should I say, Liverpool!

One day, completely out of the blue, I got the privilege of driving a Rolls Royce. This was in the early eighties and I was working at Oxenholme as usual and we had a passenger train from Harwich Parkeston Quay to Glasgow, which conveyed on the rear, three large vans containing motor cars which belonged to passengers travelling on the train. Just as it was about to depart, we noticed smoke bellowing out from underneath one of these vans. On examination, we found it was a hot axle and would have to be detached. We had the not so nice job of informing the owners of the three cars concerned, that their cars would be transferred onto another van, which we had to locate and travel north on the next available train. Needless to say, they were none too happy. The train left and the van was in the siding awaiting a replacement one to arrive from Carlisle. When this arrived we coupled it onto the disabled van, opened the end doors on both vans to enable the cars to be driven through. My boss, Kenny Harper drove the first one through and I the second, which just happened to be a chocolate coloured Rolls Royce complete with handmade leather luggage in the back. I slid slowly into the driver's seat, turned the ignition, it purred into life and I slowly drove it carefully along into the next van. I looked round to see my boss driving a Ford Escort and could only smile!

Another humorous incident I recollect, concerned an Irish lady who appeared on the platform at Oxenholme with seven children, all her own as she had so proudly informed me, ranging in age from about two to thirteen years, plus twice the amount of luggage one would normally expect, including two push chairs and asked if I could possibly assist her to board the train. Without hesitation, I was only too happy to oblige and having done so, the train set off on its way southwards. About an hour later the supervisor rang me from Lancaster in a highly agitated state. He informed me that he had this same Irish lady with all the children in his office crying her eyes out and telling him that she had lost a little three year old boy. They had held the train in Lancaster for about an hour, while they searched it but all to no avail and the mother was beside herself.

The supervisor asked me if I could check my station to see if he was still there. The station at this time was deserted and I told him so. No sooner had I said this and put the phone down, when a person came running to the booking office window and shouted, "There's a little boy having the time of his life, running through water from a tap he had turned on in the gents toilet." I ran down and was met by the sight of this little toddler wet from head to foot and laughing his head off, unaware of all the trouble and heartbreak he was causing!

I quickly retrieved him, much to his annoyance and ran back with him to the office, telling the clerk to ring and tell Lancaster that we had him safe and well. We then contacted the police at Kendal, told them the situation and they kindly took him to Lancaster for us, to reunite him with the rest of his family. British Rail had booked them all into a hotel for the night, at British Rail's expense, owing to the fact that by the time the boy had been found, all the trains had gone to where she was requiring to go. Later we received a nice thank you letter from a very grateful mother.

One hot summer's afternoon in June in the 1990's, I had just started my late shift, when a train arrived and off came a party of approximately two hundred boy scouts, plus about ten masters and there to pick them up outside the station, were four large buses and a large van. We watched them all piling on the buses wondering where they were going to stay the night, only to soon to find out because about twenty of the older ones led by a scout master, marched into our parcel office to collect their tents and their poles etc, to be told by yours truly, that for some unknown reason they had not arrived. Of course, the leader was rather annoyed!

He informed us, in no uncertain terms that this consignment of equipment had been dispatched from Reading a week ago, in ample time for it to arrive in readiness for collection by his party on arrival at Oxenholme, enroute to their camp site in the Yorkshire Dales. He did not, however, produce any written receipt at the time, which I thought was a little odd, but I did not pursue the matter because as you can imagine tempers and patience were beginning to get a little heated and frayed. I myself, after a few more trains had arrived and still no camping gear, was by now becoming only too aware, just how serious the situation was going to be. As the leader so rightly pointed out, here he was with two hundred scouts stuck out in the wilds of the countryside with no shelter for the night! Well, not quite, but nevertheless, it was quite plain that as I was the immediate representative for British Rail, it was my job to try and arrange to find some company in the Lake District or surrounding area, who would hire out tenting equipment and then provide transport to get it out to them. It was obvious that he had no intention whatsoever of paying for all this.

On the authority of my area manager, I went ahead and ordered at British Rail's expense about twenty large tents, from a firm at Windermere for the week and then I had to arrange for one of the van drivers, Syd Rumney, one of our own British Rail van drivers to turn out to run them to their site, which was a good two hours' journey away. This was a Saturday night so I wasn't too popular. Goodness knows how much it all cost but I know my area manager was not very pleased when he received the bill from the hire firm, plus the cost of the vehicle, not to mention my overtime, as I didn't get finished until 1.30 am.

The week went by and I never did actually see them going back to Reading the following Saturday but I was told, they had all thanked us for the tents, which they said were far better than theirs and for everything we had done. A few weeks later we found out that the scout master who had been responsible for dispatching the camping equipment at Reading had told the railway people there, to consign it to Abergavenny, in Wales. Obviously, he was under the impression they were going to be camping in the Brecon Beacons, with the result that the equipment had gone there. I often wondered what the scout master put in his letter to our area manager. I should imagine, it was one of embarrassment but to be fair, I did receive a most apologetic letter from him and a cheque for £10, to get myself and staff a drink on him, which we did with the greatest of pleasure!

Having worked at places such as Morecambe and eventually coming back to Oxenholme I did find a different kind of traveller. Morecambe passengers were mainly day trippers out of East Lancashire, Leeds and Bradford, whereas at Oxenholme, you got more tourists travelling here from all over the world. When first I came to Oxenholme, it was mainly Americans but in my last years more noticeably, Japanese and Chinese, all of whom were very seasoned travellers. You only had to explain which platform or a time of train to them once and they understood immediately.

We used to have our regular customers whom we got to know and this concerns one who owned a Burmese mountain dog called, 'Treacle'. His owner, Val Brennand, used to bring him every morning onto the platform when she used to wave her daughter off on the train to attend school, at Lancaster. This particular morning, for whatever reason, she had left 'Treacle' in the car. After walking down the subway talking to Peter Johnson and myself she left to go to her car. A few minutes later, she came running back, saying both 'Treacle' and car had disappeared! We ran back down the slope only to discover that her car, which she had left parked on the steep hill outside the station, was now in the hedge at the bottom. 'Treacle' had come to no harm and was lying curled up on the back seat, wondering what all the commotion was all about. On closer examination we found that the handbrake had been released and we assumed the culprit was none other than our four legged friend. The car seemed to be none the worse but 'Treacle' was never left in charge of it ever again!

I go to a driver and guards' reunion every year and I just sit and listen and enjoy the stories and humour that abound, especially from some of the more senior members who can reminisce about the Second World War years when they were just young firemen. One particular incident which occurred during the war became hair raising to say the least. Their train was loaded with ammunition and a very heavy train at that. It was bound for a port in southern England to be shipped to foreign parts. The night was wet, cold and quite wild as they approached Shap summit, they had began the descent to Oxenholme, when they became aware the brakes were not responding to the driver's needs. Driver and fireman both realized what had happened, as they hurtled down towards Oxenholme and due to the weight of the train and its contents, all they could do was pray that every signal would be off, showing green. Fortunately, their prayers were answered and they went through Oxenholme with a great sigh of relief, after which they eventually managed to stop it under its own steam. The driver said, that they often shuddered to think what destruction this would have caused if they had been required to stop. He did not think Oxenholme Station or the village itself would have been standing today. I then began to realise how brave these men were to be in charge of such lethal trains in those troubled days but being the calibre of men they were, they made light of such an incident.

Group photo of staff at Oxenholme in the early 1980's
Back row, left to right, John Cottam, Alec Chapman, Peter Johnstone, Geoff King,
Jimmy Brunskill, Malcolm Hogg and Dick Whiteside.
Front row, left to right, Ernie Lofthouse, Dorothy Burrow, Ken Bateson
and Christine Wilkinson.   Picture by Harold Bowtell

The wrecked electric truck that had been left on the line at Oxenholme by vandals
on 26/27 August 1987 and caught by the buffers of a passing train during the night
and thrown back onto the platform.   Jay Hartley

Picture taken of me when 1 was awarded 'The British Rail Superstaff Award' in 1988, at Oxenholme Station. Left to right, Ken Harper (Operations Assistant, South Cumbria); Archie McLuckie (Assistant Area Manager of British Rail, Cumbria); John Moorhouse (Secretary of the Transport Users' Consultavie Committee), myself and Mrs Olvie Clarke (Chairman of the TUCC) presenting me with the large luxury hamper.   By kind permission of the Lakeland Echo

Yours truly on Oxenholme Station, on No 1 platform in 1991.

Another tale the old chaps told me is quite amusing. A number of them were members of the Home Guard or Dad's Army as we know them today. Well, of course, being railwaymen their duties were primarily the responsibility of patrolling the railway lines in their area. On this particular night, they were marching in single file, on the side of the line over Lambrigg viaduct, when a loud explosion occurred. They all threw themselves to the ground and lay there waiting for the next explosion which never came. After a while, they thought it was safe to continue so they marched on. They then noticed the chap in front had a haversack on his back and it was leaking profusely. It was then discovered that he had a vacuum flask in his bag and that had exploded, hence the explanation for them suspecting they had come under attack and that was the only bit of excitement they had that night!

We had another driver, who always pretended he was an American. If a passenger asked him a question, depending on how he felt, he would answer them either in a 'Texas drawl', or a typical New York accent and if you were not sure what accent it was, he would take a great delight in telling you and if you met him outside work, you would really have taken him for an American. He was absolutely fanatical about the country, he was a single man and had travelled quite extensively there and knew what he was talking about. He certainly fooled a lot of people, his home town was Carlisle no less and he could revert back to his native tongue without too much trouble!

One character, whom I worked with, would contradict everything anyone said, even down to the speaking clock getting it wrong and his watch of course was right. The innumerable times he would say, "I'm going to stop those boys riding their cycles down the subways which are for 'Presbyterians only'," and the more we tried to point out, "Did you mean pedestrians?" He just would not be told!

During the last few years of my career with the railways, some remarkable machines have been invented. One of these was called an automatic train reporting or ATR for short. This enabled you to key in the reporting number of a train, after which it gave you the departure time, how many coaches it had on, the engine number, the composition of the train, where the first class carriages were, buffet and dining facilities and second classes were situated. With only using the one key, it would tell you what time it had actually departed and if late, what reason and then all the way up the line, it would tell you where the train had got to, how it was doing for time and so on. A really marvellous machine, a great help all round.

I mentioned train reporting numbers when keying in details for information on that particular train's progress. We, as railwaymen, never spoke in terms of the 0630 ex London, we referred to this train as 1S.47, the '1' meaning a class one train, the 'S' meaning it was a Scottish bound train and the '47' being the number of the train itself.

The ticket machines they have now in booking offices are all capable of issuing any kind of ticket that is available, plus sleeper and seat reservations, also for cash or credit cards.

Also now, if a train becomes very late on its journey for any reason at all, the first large station it arrives at a team of people will join it called, 'Customer Assistance Teams' (CATS for short). These people are equipped with mobile phones and they go right along the train asking people if this delay is going to cause them problems, if so, what kind and allowing the passengers to contact anyone they need to inform of this delay and generally assist the passengers in any way possible, connections etc.

During the last years I worked at Oxenholme we were fortunate in winning three prizes. The first in 1986, we collected 1st prize for 'Best Station' in the Carlisle area and received a framed certificate.

The second was in 1988, when I personally was awarded 'The British Rail Superstaff Award', by the Transport Users Consultative Committee for our region, for my high standard of service given to the travelling public. Nominations for this had been sent in by my regular travellers from Oxenholme. Mrs Olive Clarke, Chairman of the TUCC presented me with a large luxury food and drinks hamper at the station. It was a lovely surprise and I felt very honoured to receive it.

Our third was in 1994, when we received the 'Best Kept Station' award at the Hilton Hotel, in London. Miss Moira Wilson, Customer Services Manager, Alec Chapman, Chief Booking Clerk at Oxenholme, and myself went down to London to receive the award, a framed certificate.

I retired on 25 March 1995, the completion of forty-seven years with the railways. I received some lovely cards, messages and gifts. Radio Cumbria came and interviewed me on their afternoon programme and the Westmorland Gazette gave me a write-up. Then it was my turn to go home and commence putting pen to paper!

Chapter Nine
BUSMAN'S HOLIDAY TO AMERICA
AND VIPs AND CELEBRITIES I HAVE MET

I have spoken on a few occasions about the Americans travelling on our trains over here and I have to say how they praised us for their comfort, speed and, yes, you might not believe this, for our punctuality. The only complaint they did have, they never knew how to open the carriage door from inside the train, they did not realise you had to pull the window down first.

About ten years ago, my wife and I had the good fortune to take a trip across the west coast of the United States of America, by train from Denver, Colorado to Las Vegas, Nevada. Not, I must add, by British Rail passes.

We flew from Gatwick to Minneapolis, where we changed planes and then flew to Denver, stayed one night and the following morning boarded this super Amtrak train called the 'California Zephyr', leaving at 8.10 am bound for Sacramento, passing through Salt Lake City, Reno, arriving Sacramento at 12.45 pm the next day. The accommodation on board was really out of this world.

My wife and I had a cabin with two single beds, wardrobe, dressing table and when we were at dinner in the evening and went back to our cabin, our bed sheets had been turned back and a miniature bottle of wine was left on our bedside tables. There was also hot coffee 'on tap' at the end of each coach all night. You could also go and watch an all night movie if you wanted. We arrived, as I said, at Sacramento, where we stayed for two days and nights, leaving then for San Francisco, spent an enjoyable two days and nights again and then on to Los Angeles where we stayed four days, finally finishing in Las Vegas for two days. Eleven day tour in all, a truly enjoyable holiday and one I will always remember!

I always believed we could learn a few things from the Americans, especially the position of the person on our trains, whom we call the senior conductor. He is the person responsible for the overall running of the train, operationally that is, meaning for instance if the train breaks down in the wilds of the countryside, he is the person they look to, to uncouple vehicles from or to the train, namely the engine. Also, he has his commercial duties to perform, collecting and issuing tickets, giving announcements of the arrival of the train at all the stations and generally looking after his passengers' problems and needs in particular.

Whereas, on the long distance trains in America, they have what they call a 'train manager' and all he was responsible for was the passenger's comfort, explaining different and interesting places the train was travelling through. He was also in charge of all the luggage in the baggage car and all the catering on the train but he did have a person in addition to himself, who was called the conductor, who was there primarily for the operational side. I wonder if Mr Branson will think about this?

Over the years I have met many personalities, VIPs and of course Prince Charles. The ones who stand out most are those who have been particularly courteous or friendly. Quite a lot of our local dignitaries used our train regularly: Lord Wakefield, Lord Cavendish, Mr Spencer Crookenden and Major R Ewart.

Lord Whitelaw travelled weekly, to and from Penrith, when he was the Northern Ireland Secretary and was always accompanied by his bodyguard. One occasion he attended a meeting at Kendal and got off the train at Oxenholme and we then realised just how tight his security actually was.

Other regulars were Suzie Hamer, who has a regular 'agony aunts' column in 'Womens Own' and Miss Anne Pierson, Director of the Brewery Arts Centre, in Kendal, another busy lady but they always found time to say hello and talk.

Mrs Olive Clarke, JP and Deputy High Sheriff of Cumbria, used to travel quite often and was always a great advocate for British Rail and in particular for the Windermere branch.

John Tovey, a well known TV celebrity chef (who used to own the 'Miller Howe Hotel' on the shores of Windermere), used to use the station quite often, when he and his staff used to travel to London to prepare banquets on various occasions. I always found him a very sincere and down to earth person and we celebrated our Silver Wedding with a meal at his hotel. On my retirement he invited us to a lovely meal there, which we gratefully accepted and enjoyed.

I saw many stars - Kenneth More, James Garner, Gabriella Sabatini, Ava Gardner, Bob Monkhouse, Anna Neagle, Spike Milligan, Edward Woodward, Mark Little and Delia Smith.

I have seen and met many famous people but perhaps the one that stands out the most, is the American, Robert Mitchum, when he came off the train. I always count myself lucky being on duty that day. As his train came in, I was walking to the rear passing the first class coaches and closing the doors that had been left open by passengers having alighted. I came to this particular door which was open and on going to close it, a rich American voice shouted out, "Hey guy, leave that, I want to get out!" I looked up to see a large figure whom I recognised immediately as Robert Mitchum, dressed in a light cream coloured suit and large stetson hat to match. Quite impressive to say the least!

Other VIPs were Jack Jones and Lady Elizabeth Barnett, of 'What's my line?' fame. I had the pleasure of meeting this lovely lady and carried her luggage for her into the waiting room from her taxi. I remember her asking, "Where's that little train come from?" This was, of course, the Windermere train. When I told her she said, "I wish I had come to Oxenholme in it. It looks more exciting than a taxi from Windermere!" She then went on to say how much she had enjoyed her visit to the Lake District.

I also had the pleasure of meeting Jean Alexander on a few occasions. She had a relation at Windermere whom she used to go and visit and was always pleasant to talk to.

Michael Foot used to travel up from London and I met him a few times. He came for a 'Wordsworth Convention' at Grasmere and was met as he came off the train. I remember one occasion when he arrived at 11.30 pm and was approached by some young 'train spotters' for his autograph and he obliged them.

I never actually met Cliff Richard but remember in the early fifties when he played a one night stand in Carlisle with the Shadows. He was staying at the County Hotel, Carlisle, which is next to the railway station and I remember seeing his car parked there at 2 am and the windscreen was covered in lip stick. That's fame for you!

Chapter Ten
THE END OF THE LINE

As I stated earlier, I left Carlisle in 1961 but I visited Carlisle Station on numerous occasions after that and noticed how a station of its size can go down in stature over the years. I visited it in 1997 and sat myself down on a seat, near platform 8 and reminisced of days gone by, especially when a train arrived. It was a hive of activity in bygone days, the wheel-tapper tapping the wheels, water hoses to all the toilets and the dining car, porters loading and unloading parcels etc. Postmen doing the same with letter mail, the fireman on the tender of the engine watching the water pouring into the tank, all 3,500 gallons of it, and of course passengers joining it and alighting, the ticket collectors examining tickets at the ticket barrier and the noise and smell of smoke and steam from the locomotives.

I remember the Silloth trains used to leave from this platform, back in the fifties, trains consisting of maybe eight non-corridor coaches, absolutely packed with people every Saturday and Sunday during the summer months, all bound for the seaside. They used to say Silloth had the most bracing air of any seaside resort in the country. Now there is grass growing between the lines and a two coach sprinter is waiting to set off on its journey, bound for Glasgow via Dumfries and Kilmarnock. Not very exciting, I must say! Time moves on and I must also.

I am now a great grandfather, all my children are married. Denise my elder daughter, married Lorne, eldest son of Bruce and Joyce Ireland of Burneside and they have built their house opposite the old level crossing cottage. They have three children, Bronte, Bradley and Benita. Bronte, the oldest, is married to David Kenny, who is carrying on the family railway tradition and started as a railwayman at Oxenholme before I left. He was promoted to booking clerk, before becoming a team leader. They have three children, our great grandchildren, Jordan, Brooke and Heidi. Bradley and his wife Helen have a son, Luke, our fourth great grandchild. Nancy is married to Jeremy, who is a dental surgeon and lives in Bwlch, near Brecon and have three children, Eleanor and twins, Harry and Nina. Stephen married Dawn and lived for a time in Perth, Australia before coming back home to Arnside to live. My twin brother Bill, married Brenda, a Carlisle girl and they have a daugher, Anne-Marie.

I am coming to the end of my story now and would like to take this opportunity to thank all the people I have met in my forty-seven years on the railway, particularly my workmates at Kendal, Morecambe, Oxenholme and Carlisle. Sadly during the writing of this book, my old friend, Alec Mayor, died on 16 October 1998. He was a great guy and as I mentioned before he knew everything there was to know about trains, he will be greatly missed. I hope that when you make your next journey by train you will take some of my memories with you and watch out for any straying 'elephants on the line!'